酢じめ
こぶ〆
なめろう
鮮魚煮付
焼魚
野菜の煮物
きんぴら
ぬた
焼き味噌
和え物
焼野菜
出汁巻き
ポテトサラダ
本日の干魚
塩から

NIHONSHU-YA • SAKEBOZU • SHUTEI ZOROME
SHUKO TAKIGIYA • AMETSUCHI • KOTARO

Tokyo Izakaya

Delicious Pub Recipes from Six Popular Tokyo Eateries

TUTTLE Publishing

Tokyo | Rutland, Vermont | Singapore

Contents

Kotaro

Ametsuchi

Shuko Takigiya

Shutei Zorome

Sakebozu

Nihonshu-ya

Across Japan, often down quiet side streets, you can find small izakayas, furnished with a counter and just a few tables. The owner takes care of everything behind the counter, doing everything on their own, from selecting the basic ingredients to creating the menu, paying careful attention to detail at every step. The dishes served at such places are often simple, yet they have great depth of flavor, and unique methods may be used to prepare the ingredients.

In this book, we have asked the owner-chefs of several popular small izakaya in Tokyo of the type described above to show us *otsumami*—small plates to go with drinks—that can be made easily in a home kitchen. Their recipes not only show how to prepare and cook the ingredients, but are also filled with points on the fundamentals of cooking that only a professional can impart. They also give tips on how to elevate your home cooking in general.

Tasty, thoughtfully prepared dishes make drinks taste so much better. If you're thinking, "What should I have with my drink today?" you will find the answer here. We hope that this book will make drinking at home that much more enjoyable.

The Izakayas and Their Chefs

Kotaro

Chef's name: Kotaro Hayashi
Chef Hayashi creates approachable, innovative dishes using classic Japanese izakaya items as his jumping-off point (page 10).

Ametsuchi

Chef's name: Miho Tsuchii
Chef Tsuchii's simply cooked dishes bring out the full character of the ingredients she uses. Their gentle flavors impart a feeling of comfort and well-being (page 30).

Shuko Takigiya

Chef's name: Hiroto Kobayashi
Chef Kobayashi's straightforward small-plate dishes adhere to a consistent foundation of excellence, regardless of the ingredient (page 50).

Shutei Zorome

Chef's name: Hisato Ono
Great attention to fine detail is evident in all aspects of the unique, fun dishes that Chef Ono creates (page 70).

Sakebozu

Chef's name: Tomo Maeda
Chef Maeda excels in the use of spices as hidden accents. His unique approach shines in his combination of ingredients and cooking methods (page 86).

Nihonshu-ya

Chef's name: Ken'ichi Takaya
Chef Takaya is filled with ideas that are novel, but not over the top. This can be seen in the way he makes Japanese and Western flavors and cooking methods harmonize with each other (page 106).

Glossary of Ingredients

Abura-age tofu
Abura-age is a deep-fried tofu pouch, available at Japanese grocery stores. A deep-fried tofu product often called "tofu puffs," available at general Asian or Chinese grocery stores, can be substituted in recipes that call for abura-age.

Aonori seaweed powder
This is a versatile ingredient that adds color and variety. Available at Japanese grocery stores or online. Use crazy salt if you can't get hold of aonori.

Bonito flakes
Called katsuobushi in Japanese, these are flakes of fermented, dried and aged skipjack tuna or bonito. It is an essential ingredient in Japanese cooking, used to make dashi or Japanese stock, and also as a garnish or topping. The size of the flakes ranges from very fine and powder-like to large, long shavings that look like wood shavings. Available at Japanese grocery stores or online.

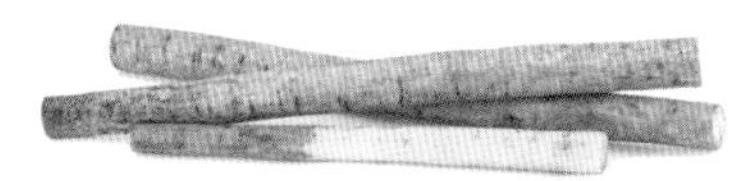

Burdock root
The distinctive crunchy texture and earthy flavor really whet the appetite. You can find burdock root for sale at East Asian grocery stores. If you can't find burdock root, carrot has a similar texture.

Cod roe
Salted spicy cod or pollack roe is called mentaiko in Japanese. It is a popular filling for onigiri rice balls, and is used often as a condiment. You can find mentaiko at well-stocked Japanese grocery stores, where it is usually sold frozen. Defrost in the refrigerator and use on the same day.

Freeze-dried tofu
Freeze dried tofu, called koya dofu in Japanese, is very healthy like regular tofu, but is surprisingly filling because of the slightly meaty, spongy texture. Available at Japanese grocery stores or online.

Karashi mustard
This hot, yellow mustard is similar to English mustard, which can be used as a substitute in the recipes in this book. "Oriental hot mustard," available in regular supermarkets, can also be used. Karashi mustard can be found in Japanese groceries, in powdered form or ready-made in a tube.

Kombu seaweed
Kombu seaweed is the thick, leathery green-brown seaweed used to make dashi or Japanese stock, the foundation of traditional Japanese cuisine. It's also used to add a shot of umami in various recipes. Kombu seaweed is always sold in dried form, and you can find it at Japanese grocery stores or online.

Mirin
Mirin, also called hon mirin, is a sweet alcoholic liquor made from rice. Although it is a beverage, nowadays it's used almost exclusively for cooking. It has a sweet taste and is often used instead of sugar in various recipes, and is a staple in Japanese kitchens. You can also find something called mirin seasoning or aji mirin, which is an alcohol-free substitute for mirin that contains sweeteners (sugar or high-fructose corn syrup), salt and monosodium glutamate. Mirin seasoning will do in a pinch, but real mirin has a better flavor. Available at Japanese and general Asian grocery stores as well as some general supermarkets.

Miso
Miso is a fermented paste made with soybeans, salt, and Aspergillus oryzae microbes. Grains such as wheat, rice or barley are often added to the mix before fermenting. The color of miso can range from a pale yellow-brown to a deep-reddish brown, almost black. Miso can be found at many regular supermarkets and health food stores as well as at Japanese groceries.

Myoga ginger
Myoga is a type of ginger bud often used as a garnish. If you can't find myoga, use thinly sliced mature ginger or fresh ginger shoots, which you may be able to find at Chinese or Thai grocery stores.

Nori seaweed

Seaweed or laver that is stretched out in sheets and dried. The best nori has a green-black color. This is the seaweed that's wrapped around sushi rolls. It's available in many regular supermarkets as well as in Japanese grocery stores.

Okara

Okara, translated as "soy pulp" or "tofu dregs," is the name for the fibrous, insoluble parts of the soybean after the soy milk has been extracted. In Japan this is available very cheaply, but elsewhere it may be hard to find. If you have a tofu maker near you, ask them if they have okara. If you make your own soy milk or tofu, you will have plenty!

Ponzu sauce

Ponzu sauce is made with a combination of citrus juice, vinegar, soy sauce, kombu seaweed and bonito flakes. It is salty, sour and packed with umami. You can substitute lemon or lime juice. Bottled ponzu sauce is available at Japanese grocery stores.

Shio kombu

Shio kombu is kombu seaweed that has been simmered until tender in a soy-sauce-based sauce. It can be used like a condiment or flavoring ingredient to add saltiness and umami. Available at Japanese grocery stores or online. If you can't find shio kombu, use crazy salt or just a pinch of ordinary salt instead.

Sesame oil

Oil made with toasted sesame seeds. It has an amber color and a rich, nutty fragrance and flavor. It's available at general Asian grocery stores.

Sesame seeds

Pre-ground sesame seeds (available at Japanese grocery stores) can be used as-is in many recipes in this book. If you can't get them pre-ground, grind up whole toasted sesame seeds roughly with a mortar and pestle or with a food mill, and store in plastic zip bags in the freezer.

Shibazuke pickles

These sour and salty pickles are made from eggplant, ginger and red shiso leaves, which give the pickle its purple color. You can find shibazuke pickles ready made at Japanese grocery stores.

Shiso leaves

Shiso is a fragrant herb that is used extensively in Japanese cooking. The leaves add a nice touch of freshness to any dish.

Do not confuse shiso leaves (Perilla frutescens var. Crispa) with Korean perilla or kkaennip (Perilla frutescens); although they look similar, Korean perilla has a stronger aniseed-like flavor. Green shiso is frillier and green on both sides, while Korean perilla has a purple tinge on the back side of the leaves. Fresh green shiso is available at well stocked Japanese grocery stores and some gourmet supermarkets. It's well worth growing your own if you can.

Soy sauce

Soy sauce comes in different types, but most widely used in Japan is koikuchi or dark soy sauce. Another type of soy sauce that is becoming more available outside of Japan is usukuchi or light soy sauce. Although the name says "light," it is actually higher in salt than dark soy sauce. Light soy sauce is used in dishes where the flavor of soy sauce is required but not the dark color. Unless specified, you can use either light or dark soy sauce in the recipes in this book.

Umeboshi pickled plums

These salt-preserved plums are related to apricots but are much tarter. They are usually salty and sour, although sometimes they are sweetened with sugar or honey. There are small, hard, crunchy ones, and ones with loose, soft flesh that can be chopped up. The recipes in this book use the latter type. Umeboshi keep for a long time. Store in a cool, dark cupboard or the refrigerator. Some lower-salt versions need to be refrigerated after opening. Available at Japanese grocery stores or online.

Water pepper leaves

Called benitade in Japanese, you may find this spicy herb with maroon and green leaves at your Japanese grocery or farmers' market.

Yuzu kosho paste

A condiment made with green chili paste and yuzu citrus peel. It has a citrusy fragrance and is quite spicy. Available at Japanese grocery stores or online.

Kotaro

Classic Recipes Beloved by All

Located on a small back street in the Shibuya district,
Kotaro is an izakaya where adults can unwind over food and
drinks. We recommend sitting at the counter
so you can watch as your food is being prepared.

Make a recipe again and again until it becomes a "go-to" dish

The most important thing for me as I cook is to observe people's faces as they eat my food. It's a cliché, but it's true: food is love. Food that is cooked from the heart relaxes you and tastes better than anything else.

Some people say that when they try to follow a recipe, it doesn't work out very well. But no one can get everything right the first time. In cooking, repetition is important. So instead of trying one new recipe after another, try making the ones you like again and again. This way the flavors will take shape and the recipes will become your own. If it doesn't go well, think about why it didn't work out and use those lessons for the next time—this is how you will improve. When people praise your cooking, you gain confidence and enjoy the process of making a dish even more.

Recipes are never totally original. They are made by someone who takes existing ingredients and arranges them in their own way. So start out by copying someone else's recipe. After you make it several times, it will become your own. Everyone grows up with a different background or in a different region, so people's tastes always vary. Even if you start out by copying someone, it's fine to change the flavors according to your preferences. And if you manage to create five dishes this way that are "your own," that's great! I think that means you have become a good cook. And by using those five dishes as a base and changing up the flavors and ingredients, you can increase your repertoire.

Memorize the cooking steps and execute them efficiently and speedily

Another important aspect of cooking is the tempo. If you try to cook by referring too closely to a cookbook, you may get the timing wrong, which may lead to overcooking things, not capturing the flavor, and so on. Memorize the steps and make them a part of you, and keep an image of the final result in your mind. Even if you can't get it right the first time, as you make it twice, three times and more, and get used to the process, you'll be able to make it speedily and without wasted effort. As for flavoring, if you overseason something, you can't undo it, so I think it's best to start by seasoning lightly, and adding more as you become familiar with the dish.

Whenever I go out to eat Western-style or Chinese-style cuisine, I have a longstanding habit of writing down the ingredients and cooking methods that intrigue me, and then incorporating them into the *washoku* (traditional Japanese) dishes I serve at my own place. Cooking is the process of putting together ingredients and cooking methods like a puzzle. For instance, when you try adding nonstandard ingredients to classic dishes, such as putting tart umeboshi plums into pork shabu-shabu hot pot, or adding tomatoes to sukiyaki beef hot pot, a different dish is born. Don't be afraid of experimenting and making mistakes, and be adventurous in trying out different combinations.

Tips from Chef Hayashi of Kotaro

1. Cook briskly and with a good rhythm

In cooking, speed is important. Instead of trying to cook while referring to a cookbook, memorize the steps in advance. Once you can make a dish quickly and efficiently, your cooking is sure to improve, too.

2. Have five "go-to" dishes

You only need to have five go-to dishes that you can say you are good at making. That will lead to increased confidence in your cooking. In order to acquire five such dishes, make the ones you like repeatedly until they become your own.

3. Combine ingredients and cooking methods

Cooking is just a matter of combining ingredients and cooking methods. Put them together like a puzzle so you can increase your repertoire. And try different cuisines! This will refine your palate so that you can create combinations that work.

Chicken and Cucumber with Sesame Dressing

The chicken in this dish is remarkably tender. The key is to not let it boil; simply cook it gently in residual heat. You'll be amazed at the delicate texture.

Serves 2

2 chicken tenders, about 3½ oz (100 g) total
1½ cups (360 ml) water
3 tablespoons + 1 teaspoon sake
1 small Japanese or Asian cucumber
Toasted sesame seeds, for garnish

FOR THE SESAME DRESSING
1½ tablespoons tahini
⅓ teaspoon grated ginger
⅓ cup (80 ml) dashi stock (see page 54)
2 teaspoons light soy sauce
2 teaspoons mirin

1 Remove the sinews from the chicken tenders. Bring about 1½ cups (360 ml) of water to a boil, then turn off the heat and add the sake. Add the chicken tenders, and leave for about 5 minutes to cook in residual heat.
2 Peel long strips from the cucumber skin to make stripes. Halve lengthwise and remove seeds. Cut into ½ inch (1 cm) wide diagonal slices.
3 Mix all the sesame dressing ingredients together.
4 Shred the chicken into bite-sized pieces with your hands. Toss the chicken and cucumber with the dressing. Arrange in a serving bowl and sprinkle with sesame seeds.

Sesame-Scented Myoga Ginger and Whitebait

This Japanese take on the classic Korean side dish *namul* is very popular at my restaurant. Use plenty of myoga ginger—about the same amount as the whitebait—and enjoy the contrasting flavors and textures.

Serves 2

3 myoga ginger buds
2 oz (60 g) whitebait
Toasted sesame oil, to taste
Salt, to taste
Toasted white sesame seeds, for garnish

1 Slice the myoga ginger into thin rounds. Let stand in a bowl of cold water for a few minutes, then drain well.
2 Combine the sliced myoga ginger and whitebait, drizzle with a little sesame oil and toss quickly. Taste and add salt if desired.
3 Arrange in a serving bowl and top with sesame seeds.

Zucchini and Onion with Tuna

Canned tuna is given a refreshing twist with tangy ponzu sauce. Don't slice the zucchini too thinly—keep it thick so you can enjoy its juicy texture to the fullest.

Serves 2

½ zucchini
Salt, for sprinkling
⅕ red or white onion
1¾ oz (50 g) tuna canned in oil
1 tablespoon ponzu soy sauce (see note below)

NOTE You can buy bottled ponzu soy sauce, but to make your own, mix equal parts soy sauce and lemon or lime juice (or any citrus juice of your choosing).

1 Peel alternating strips from the zucchini skin to make stripes, then cut the zucchini into ¼ inch (5 mm) thick slices. Sprinkle with a little salt and let stand for 5 minutes. Massage briefly, rinse in cold water and squeeze out the excess moisture.

2 Slice the onion thinly and let stand in a bowl of cold water for a few minutes, then drain well.

3 Drain the tuna and combine with the ponzu soy sauce in a bowl. Add the zucchini and onion. Mix to combine, then taste, adding a little more ponzu soy sauce if needed.

Octopus and Celery Ohitashi with Sesame

Ohitashi is a classic Japanese vegetable side dish. In this version, shio kombu (dried and seasoned kombu seaweed) is used to add instant umami and saltiness. I recommend using very finely shredded shio kombu if you can find it.

Serves 2

1¾ oz (50 g) cooked octopus (see note below)
1 celery stalk, with leaves
Salt, for sprinkling
Pinch finely shredded shio kombu
1 tablespoon vegetable oil or light (not toasted) sesame oil
Toasted white sesame seeds, for garnish

NOTE You can use any white fish sashimi in place of the cooked octopus.

1 Slice the octopus into thin rounds.
2 Remove the tough outer strings from the celery stalk and cut into thin diagonal slices, reserving the leaves. Sprinkle with salt and let stand for about 5 minutes. Squeeze the celery tightly to remove excess moisture.
3 Coarsely chop the celery leaves and blanch in boiling water for a few seconds. Drain well and squeeze to remove excess moisture. If needed, shred the shio kombu finely.
4 Combine the octopus, sliced celery and celery leaves in a bowl with the shredded shio kombu. Drizzle with the oil and toss briefly. Arrange on a serving plate and sprinkle with toasted sesame seeds.

Tofu in Broth with Spiced Cod Roe

This recipe is so easy that anyone can make it successfully, as long as the ingredients are on hand. Try it with udon noodles in place of the tofu, too!

Serves 2

1 large sac spiced cod roe (karashi mentaiko)
2 tablespoons cornstarch or potato starch dissolved in 6 tablespoons water
1 block silken tofu, about 10½ oz (300 g)
Chopped green onion, for garnish

FOR THE BROTH
1½ cups (350 ml) dashi stock (see page 54)
1 tablespoon + 1 teaspoon sake
1 teaspoon mirin
1 teaspoon light soy sauce

1 Make a long slit down one side of the cod roe sac and scrape out all the roe. Combine the broth ingredients in a small earthenware pot (*donabe*) or heavy saucepan and heat. When the broth comes to a boil, add two-thirds of the roe and mix. Add the starch dissolved in water and stir to thicken.
2 Cut the tofu into bite-sized pieces and add to the soup. Put the lid on and simmer over low heat. When the tofu is heated through, add the remaining roe and sprinkle with the green onion.

Oysters Marinated in Oil

To make this dish a success, prepare the oysters with care. Blanching them will cut any fishy odors, but be sure not to overcook lest they get tough. These oysters will keep for about 10 days in the refrigerator if it completely immersed in the marinating oil.

Serves 2

20 shelled oysters
Grated daikon radish to cover the oysters
2 cups (500 ml) water
¾ cup (180 ml) soy sauce
6 tablespoons vegetable oil
3 tablespoons light olive oil

NOTE 1 The flavorful soy sauce that is drained off the oysters can be used in other dishes, such as fried rice or stir-fried vegetables.
NOTE 2 If there isn't enough oil to completely immerse the oysters, add more, keeping the 2:1 ratio between vegetable oil and olive oil.

1 Combine the oysters and grated daikon radish in a bowl and mix gently to remove any surface impurities from the oysters. Rinse under running water and pat dry. Heat the 2 cups of water in a pan to just below boiling, then reduce the heat to low. Add the oysters, removing them as soon as they change color.
2 Rinse the pan and return the oysters to it, along with the soy sauce. Cook over high heat for 1 to 2 minutes, shaking the pan the whole time. When the oysters are coated with the soy sauce and begin to get plump, turn off the heat. Drain the oysters in a colander, reserving the liquid (see Note 1), and allow to cool. Transfer to an airtight container and refrigerate until completely chilled.
3 Add the vegetable oil and olive oil to the container (see Note 2) and refrigerate overnight.

Chicken Gizzards and Green Beans with Sesame

The key to this dish is to carefully cut away the tough membranes of the gizzards, then marinate them to add flavor. Slice the gizzards thinly and combine them with green beans for a great combination of tastes and textures.

Serves 2

3 pairs chicken gizzards or giblets
1 tablespoon sake
1 tablespoon soy sauce
5 green beans

FOR THE SESAME SAUCE
5 tablespoons toasted sesame seeds
1¾ oz tablespoons tahini
3 teaspoons sugar
3 teaspoons soy sauce

1 Gizzards usually come in pairs that are connected with a white membrane. Cut them apart, then carefully remove all the white membrane. Slice each gizzard into 3 to 4 pieces.
2 Combine the sake and soy sauce in a bowl and add the gizzards. Marinate for about 10 minutes. Drain, then stir-fry in a skillet over low heat.
3 Trim the green beans, blanch in boiling water and cut each one into 3 or 4 pieces.
4 To make the sesame sauce, place the toasted sesame seeds in a mortar and grind them up. Add the remaining sauce ingredients and mix. (Alternatively, you can blend everything together in a food processor.)
5 Put 1 to 2 tablespoons of the sesame sauce in a bowl and thin with a little water. Add the chicken gizzards and green beans and mix. The leftover sesame sauce can be stored, tightly covered, in the refrigerator.

Simmered Manila Clams

If you blanch clams briefly before simmering them, any fishy flavors will be eliminated and the simmering liquid will remain clear. This way, the dish will look as good as it tastes.

Serves 2

3 cups (700 ml) water
9 oz (250 g) shelled Manila clams or littleneck clams
¾ inch (2 cm) length ginger, finely slivered, for garnish

FOR THE SIMMERING SAUCE
⅔ cup (150 ml) dashi stock (see page 54)
1 tablespoon + 2 teaspoons sake
1 tablespoon + 2 teaspoons mirin
1 tablespoon + 2 teaspoons soy sauce

1 Heat the water in a saucepan. Just before it comes to a full boil, turn down the heat and add the shelled clams. When they change color, drain them in a colander and rinse quickly under running water.
2 Combine the simmering sauce ingredients in a pan over medium heat. When it comes to a boil, add the clams and the slivered ginger, reserving a teaspoon of the ginger for garnish. Return to a boil, skim off any scum and simmer over low heat for about 1 minute. Turn off the heat and leave until cool so that the clams absorb the liquid.
3 Arrange on a serving plate and sprinkle the reserved ginger on top.
4 Keep leftovers covered in the refrigerator, and eat within 4 days.

Pork Shabu-Shabu Hot Pot with Umeboshi Plum

For a clear, clean-tasting soup, blanch the pork briefly before you add it. The umeboshi adds piquancy to the broth. Be sure to use a sour umeboshi rather than a sweet one.

Serves 2

2 cups (500 ml) water
3½ oz (100 g) very thinly sliced pork loin
⅛ head iceberg lettuce

FOR THE BROTH
2⅓ cups (550 ml) dashi stock (see page 54)
2 teaspoons sake
2 teaspoons mirin
2 teaspoons light soy sauce
Salt
4 inch (10 cm) length kombu seaweed
1 umeboshi plum

1 Combine the broth ingredients in a small earthenware pot (*donabe*) or heavy cast-iron pot. Heat until boiling, then turn the heat down low and simmer for 10 minutes to transfer the flavors of the kombu seaweed and umeboshi to the broth.

2 Heat the water in a separate pan. Just before it comes to a full boil, add the pork slices. When the meat changes color, remove it immediately from the water and drain in a colander. Cut the lettuce into large bite-sized wedges.

3 Add the pork and lettuce to the broth and heat through.

Marinated Mackerel

The hot marinating liquid is poured over raw vegetables so that they retain their crisp texture while being cooked. That tender crunch is a major feature of this classic dish. Any leftovers can be kept refrigerated for a couple of days.

Serves 2

4 mackerel, filleted, about 1 lb (450g) total (large sardines or another type of mackerel may be used)
Flour, for dusting
Vegetable oil, for frying
1 large celery stalk
⅓ medium carrot
¼ onion

FOR THE MARINADE
1½ cups (350 ml) dashi stock (see page 54)
3 tablespoons rice vinegar
3 tablespoons mirin
3 tablespoons soy sauce
1⅔ tablespoons sugar
1 red chili pepper, stem and seeds removed

1 Cut the mackerel fillets in half or into bite-sized pieces and dust lightly with flour. Heat the vegetable oil to 360°F (180°C) and deep fry the fish pieces until crispy.
2 Remove the tough outer strings from the celery stalk and cut into diagonal slices about ¼ inch (5 mm) wide. Cut the carrot into short strips and slice the onion thinly.
3 Place the fried fish in a bowl and arrange the vegetables on top.
4 Combine all the marinade ingredients in a pan and bring to a boil. Immediately pour the hot marinade over the vegetables and fish. Cover the bowl with cling film while still hot and let stand until cool so that the ingredients absorb the flavor of the marinade.
5 Allow the marinade to cool completely, and then refrigerate for at least an hour before serving.

Deep-Fried Sea Eel with Shibazuke Tartar Sauce

Instead the usual cucumber pickles in my tartar sauce, I use shibazuke pickles, which contain cucumber, eggplant, ginger and purple shiso. This adds a beautiful color and a Japanese twist, making the tartar sauce a highlight of this dish. Deep-fry the sea eel (*anago* in Japanese) twice so it becomes tender and fluffy. Instead of eel, you can substitute mackerel or other oily fish.

Serves 2

1 sea eel (anago), filleted (mackerel or salmon may be substituted)
Salt and pepper, to taste
Flour, for dusting
1 egg, beaten
Panko breadcrumbs, for dredging
Vegetable oil, for frying
Lemon wedges

FOR THE SHIBAZUKE TARTAR SAUCE
½ onion, finely minced
3 hard-boiled eggs
3½ oz (100 g) shibazuke pickles, finely chopped
5 tablespoons mayonnaise
Black pepper

1 Make the shibazuke tartar sauce: rinse the minced onion in cold water and drain well. Crush the hard-boiled egg yolks with a fork and chop the whites finely. Combine all the tartar sauce ingredients, including the eggs, in a bowl.
2 Put the eel fillet in a colander and pour boiling water over it, then immediately plunge into cold water. Drain, transfer to a cutting board and scrape the surface to remove any sliminess. (This step is not necessary if you are using a fish other than eel.)
3 Pat the eel dry and sprinkle it with salt and pepper. Dust it with flour, dip it in the beaten egg and dredge it in the panko breadcrumbs.
4 Heat the vegetable oil to 360°F (180°C) and deep-fry the eel pieces until lightly browned. Remove them from the oil, leave for about 5 minutes to continue cooking with residual heat, then return them to the oil until golden brown and crispy. Drain on paper towels.
5 Arrange the fried eel pieces on a plate with the shibazuke tartar sauce. Spritz with the lemon at the table.

About Shibazuke Tartar Sauce

This colorful tartar sauce goes well with all kinds of deep-fried food, such as fried chicken or other types of fried fish. Although it is quite pale when you first make it, it turns a deeper pink as time passes. It will keep in the refrigerator for about a week.

Simmered Beef Tendon and Winter Melon

The beef tendon is blanched first, then rinsed to remove any surface impurities before being slowly simmered until tender. The key is to cook it thoroughly before seasoning it. Both the tendon and the melon will melt in your mouth.

Serves 2

10 oz (300 g) beef tendon
1/8 winter melon
Green part of 1 leek, or of 1 large or 2 medium green onions
3/4 inch (2 cm) length ginger, sliced
Zest of 1 green yuzu fruit or lemon, for garnish

FOR THE SIMMERING LIQUID
2 1/4 cups (540 ml) dashi stock (see page 54)
6 tablespoons sake
1 1/2 tablespoons light soy sauce
1 1/2 tablespoons mirin
4 inch (10 cm) strip kombu seaweed
Salt, to taste

NOTE 1 Parboiled beef tendon will keep in the refrigerator for 5 to 6 days, so you can cook a larger amount to keep on hand. It's great in udon dishes, various simmered dishes, curries and so on.
NOTE 2 Try to remove as little peel as possible so that the winter melon retains its attractive green color. To preserve the color even better, sprinkle the peeled surfaces with a little baking soda before cutting.

1 Put the beef tendon in a large pan with plenty of water. Bring to a boil, drain into a colander and rinse briefly. Return the beef tendon to the pan with fresh water and add the leek or green onions and sliced ginger. Bring to a boil over high heat, then skim off any scum and continue to boil for about 3 hours or until tender, adding additional water as needed. (See Note 1 below.)
2 Cut the winter melon into 1 inch (2.5 cm) cubes and peel thinly (see Note 2 below). Bring a separate pot of water to a boil, add the winter melon and simmer over low heat for about 20 minutes. Drain.
3 Drain the beef tendon. Combine in a separate pan with all the simmering liquid ingredients and bring to a boil. Reduce the heat to medium and leave to simmer for about 20 minutes.
4 Add the simmered winter melon to the beef tendon and continue to simmer for about 10 minutes to blend the flavors. Arrange in serving bowls and top with grated yuzu or lemon zest.

Ametsuchi

Simple Preparations that Highlight the Ingredients

Ametsuchi is a small, quiet *obanzai-ya*—a restaurant that serves homey dishes—behind an old-fashioned sliding door. The restaurant's motto is "A nightcap with vegetables."

Add seasonal items to your repertoire

This happens to be the core concept behind Ametsuchi, but if you are going to cook I believe it's much more fun if you incorporate seasonal items. Take that Japanese standby, potato salad, for example, and try adding some grilled sweet corn to it in the summer. Or if you're making a simple tofu dish and clams are in season, try adding some sake-steamed clams. By simply adding seasonal ingredients to the recipes you make all the time, you can turn a regular dish into something special. While it's fine to challenge yourself by trying new recipes, using seasonal ingredients is an effortless way to add new flavors.

In a similar vein, simply changing the dashi stock you use is an easy way to impart new flavors to favorite dishes. Our basic dashi stock is made from kombu seaweed and bonito flakes, but when I want to lighten up a vegetable dish, or when the vegetables themselves have strong umami, I use a light dashi stock made with kombu only. Vegetable dishes in particular are often much better when made with a simple kombu dashi stock that allows the diner to fully appreciate the flavors of the vegetables. Kombu dashi without bonito flakes also works well with fish dishes. But *oden* (a winter dish of simmered fish cakes and vegetables) is a dish that I feel needs a bit more umami, so I add *niboshi* (dried sardines) to the basic kombu dashi.

Add kombu seaweed to simmered dishes

Many home cooks find that making dashi stock is a bother, but you can simply add a piece of kombu to any simmered dish and cook it together with the other ingredients.

Tips from Chef Tsuchii of Ametsuchi

1. Use seasonal ingredients to enhance your favorite recipes

When seasonal ingredients are on your table, life feels more abundant! Incorporating seasonal ingredients into your favorite go-to dishes is also an easy way to create something new without the worry of trying out an unfamiliar recipe.

2. Simmer the kombu seaweed with the other ingredients instead of making stock

When you don't have time to make a dashi stock, just add a piece of kombu to the pan where you are simmering the main ingredients. The umami of the kombu will be released as it cooks. Don't throw away the kombu you use to make dashi stock, either; you should keep it to add to other dishes.

3. Combine umami-rich ingredients

The typical ingredients used to create traditional Japanese dashi stock include kombu seaweed, bonito flakes and *niboshi* (dried sardines). But you can make dashi stock from many other umami-rich ingredients, such as meat, mush-rooms and tomatoes.

For example, if you are making simmered veg-etables with clams, just put water and a piece of kombu in the pan with the vegetables, allow it to cook for a while, add the clams and you're done. Don't throw away the kombu, bonito flakes and other ingredients you've used to make dashi stock. Keep them in the refrigera-tor to use in simmered dishes or stews the next day. Kombu that's been used to make dashi is particularly good for giving simmered fish dishes a great umami boost. Although con-ventional wisdom says that you shouldn't cook kombu with too much heat since it can impart some undesirable flavors, if you're cooking at home, I don't think you don't have to worry too much about that.

People around me are always surprised when they learn that my cooking is centered around such simple ingredients. Another characteristic of my food is that I don't add much sweetness, because I want to bring out the natural flavors of the main ingredients. To make up for that, though, I purposely use in-gredients that are rich in umami to add depth and variety to the flavors. For example, if I put a piece of kombu in water, bring it to a boil, add mushrooms, tomato and thinly cut pork, all those ingredients release lots of umami. Thus, only a little salt and perhaps a drizzle of soy sauce are needed to make this simple dish totally delicious. The semi-dried fish known as *himono* has very strong umami, too. I grill the fish lightly and make a dashi stock from it—it's so flavorful that you only need to add sake and vegetables to make a delicious and satisfying simmered dish.

In short, a good dashi stock can create great flavors without the need for sake or soy sauce, and it will really allow you to savor the taste of the main ingredients.

Mizuna Greens Ohitashi

Ohitashi—a dish that usually refers to blanched vegetables in a dashi-based sauce—is a staple of my cooking. It is the quintessential Japanese-style salad. The word *hitashi* comes from the verb *hitasu*, which means "to soak," as the greens are soaked in a flavorful sauce.

Serves 2

1 liter (500 ml) water
½ teaspoon salt
Small bunch mizuna greens, about 3½ oz (100 g)
½ piece deep-fried tofu (abura-age)
Finely shaved bonito flakes, for garnish

FOR THE SAUCE
¾ cup (180 ml) dashi stock (see page 54)
2 teaspoons sake
2 teaspoons light soy sauce

1 Combine the water and the salt in a saucepan and bring to a boil. Blanch the mizuna greens briefly, then drain and plunge into cold water. Drain the greens and squeeze out the moisture. Cut into 1½ inch (4 cm) lengths.
2 Slice the deep-fried tofu into fairly thin strips.
3 Combine all the sauce ingredients in a saucepan over medium heat. Add the sliced deep-fried tofu. When it comes to a boil, turn off the heat and allow to cool. Mix in the mizuna greens and refrigerate for at least 3 hours.
4 Arrange on a serving plate and top with the bonito flakes.

Spinach Ohitashi with Sesame

This dish traditionally has a very sweet sauce, but my version uses a sauce base of dashi stock and soy sauce with sesame added for a simple yet robust flavor.

Serves 2

4 cups (500 ml) water
½ teaspoon salt
Small bunch spinach, about 3½ oz (100 g)
1 oz (30 g) beech mushrooms (shimeji)
Small piece carrot, about ½ oz (15 g)
2 tablespoons toasted sesame seeds
Salt, to taste

FOR THE SAUCE
¾ cup (180 ml) dashi stock (see page 54)
2 teaspoons sake
2 teaspoons light soy sauce

1 Combine the water and salt in a saucepan and bring to a boil. Blanch the spinach briefly, then drain and plunge into cold water. Drain and squeeze out the moisture.

2 Cut the blanched spinach into 1½ inch (4 cm) lengths. Remove the tough stem ends from the beech mushrooms and divide the clump into individual mushrooms. Cut the carrot into 1½ inch (4 cm) long matchsticks.

3 Combine all the sauce ingredients with the mushrooms and carrot in a saucepan over medium heat. Cook until the carrot is tender, then turn off the heat and allow to cool. Add the spinach, toss to coat in the sauce and refrigerate for about 1 hour.

4 Grind the sesame seeds in a mortar until the seeds are half crushed. Drain the vegetables briefly and mix with the sesame seeds before serving.

Chrysanthemum Greens with Tofu Sauce

This classic dish with tofu is known as *shira-ae* in Japanese. Either silken or firm tofu is used, depending on the ingredients. With vegetables, I usually use firm tofu to get a fuller flavor, and with fruit I use smooth, creamy silken tofu.

Serves 2

Piece firm tofu, about 3½ oz (100 g)
Small bunch chrysanthemum greens or garland chrysanthemum, about 5 oz (150 g), (watercress, chard or collard greens may be substituted)
4 cups (500 ml) water
½ teaspoon salt, plus more to taste
6 tablespoons dashi stock (see page 54)
1 teaspoon sake
1 teaspoon light soy sauce
4–5 walnut halves
1 teaspoon ground sesame seeds

1 Wrap the tofu in paper towels or a clean kitchen towel and set a weight on top. Allow to sit so that the water drains off, until its volume is reduced by about half.
2 Remove the leaves from the stems of the greens and thinly slice the stems diagonally. Combine the water and salt and bring to a boil. Blanch the greens briefly, then drain and plunge into cold water. Drain again and squeeze out excess moisture.
3 Combine the dashi, sake and soy sauce in a bowl. Add the greens, stir to coat and let stand for about 15 minutes.
4 Toast the walnuts in a dry skillet until they are very lightly browned and aromatic. Chop coarsely.
5 Put the drained tofu in a bowl and mash roughly. Stir in salt to taste. Drain the greens briefly and stir into the tofu. Add the walnuts and sesame seeds and mix everything together.

Komatsuna Greens with Nori Seaweed

This dish is based on a traditional Japanese dish called *nibitashi*, where the greens are cooked in the sauce and cooled in it. Komatsuna greens work especially well with this method, but they taste a little bland, so I have added nori seaweed, along with a traditional preserved soybean product made in Niigata Prefecture called *uchimame*. If you can't find uchimame, you can omit it or substitute edamame beans; the dish will still be tasty.

Serves 2

Small bunch komatsuna greens, about 3½ oz (100 g) (spinach or chard leaves may be substituted)
⅓ oz (10 g) uchimame (optional), or a few edamame beans
⅛ sheet of nori seaweed (about 2 x 4 inches or 5 x 10 cm)

FOR THE SAUCE
¾ cup (180 ml) dashi stock (see page 54)
2 teaspoons sake
2 teaspoons light soy sauce

1 Cut the komatsuna or other greens into 1½ inch (4 cm) long pieces. Rinse the uchimame and soak in water for about 10 minutes.
2 Drain the uchimame, if using. Combine all the sauce ingredients and the uchimame in a saucepan over medium heat. Cook for about 5 minutes. Add the greens, removing the pan from the heat as soon as they are wilted. Allow to cool so that the greens absorb the flavors of the sauce.
3 Tear the nori seaweed into small pieces and scatter over the greens before serving.

Grilled Chicken Marinated in Sake Lees

You can cook this a day after marinating, but it's even more delicious if you can marinate for a week and allow the flavor of the meat to mature.

Serves 2

2 boneless chicken thighs, about 7 oz (200 g) total
1 teaspoon coarse salt
Inner core of a celery heart, finely slivered, for garnish

FOR THE MARINADE
5 oz (150 g) sake lees (see note below)
2 tablespoons sake
2 tablespoons mirin
2 tablespoons soy sauce
1 teaspoon sugar

1 Remove any excess fat from the chicken thighs. Make horizontal cuts in the thicker parts of the thigh and open them up to even out the thickness. Rub the coarse salt into both sides of the chicken and let stand for about 2 hours, then rinse the meat and pat dry.
2 Combine all marinade ingredients, mixing well. Spread on both sides of the chicken, putting more on the non-skin side than the skin side. Wrap in cling film and refrigerate for at least a day, but no more than a week.
3 When you are ready to cook the chicken, wipe the marinade off the meat and grill on both sides until browned. Cut into bite-sized pieces, and serve with a heap of slivered celery alongside.

NOTE Sake lees (sake *kasu*), a byproduct of sake production, are packed with umami and redolent of sake. The alcohol acts as a preservative, allowing you to marinate the chicken days in advance. Sake lees may be available at a Japanese market—or you may be able to buy them directly from a sake brewery if you live near one!

Sake-Simmered Sardines

These simmered sardines are delicious hot or cold, and they lend themselves to many variations. Try adding them to a salad with lots of vegetables, dressed simply with olive oil and lemon. The sardines will keep in the refrigerator for 3 or 4 days.

Serves 2

3 to 4 fresh sardines, 7 oz (200 g) total
1 tsp coarse salt
Green part of 1 leek or 1 large green onion
¾ inch (2 cm) length ginger, peeled and thinly sliced
4 green shiso leaves, cut into ribbons
2 myoga ginger buds, thinly sliced
Lemon wedge

FOR THE SIMMERING SAUCE
1⅔ cups (400 ml) dashi stock (see page 54)
1 piece of kombu seaweed left over from making dashi stock, optional
6 tablespoons sake
1 teaspoon salt

1 Cut the heads off the sardines. Make a slit through the belly side and scrape out the innards with a knife. Rinse out the blood and remaining innards and pat dry. Sprinkle with the coarse salt and let stand for 30 minutes, then rinse and pat dry.

2 Combine all the simmering sauce ingredients in a pan over very low heat. Add the leek or green onion and the ginger, then lay the sardines on top. Simmer slowly for 30 minutes. Turn off the heat and let stand until cool.

3 Arrange the sardines on serving plates and top with the shredded shiso leaves and myoga ginger. Place a lemon wedge on the side and drizzle with lemon juice before eating.

Simmered Tofu

Freeze-dried tofu, called *koya dofu* in Japan, is usually simmered in a rather sweet sauce. Here I have cut down on the sweetness to bring out the flavor of the dashi stock that permeates the spongy tofu. Add the soy sauce at the end for maximum fragrance.

Serves 2

2 squares freeze-dried tofu (koya dofu)
2 teaspoons light soy sauce
3–4 blanched snow peas

FOR THE SAUCE
1¼ cups (300 ml) dashi stock (see page 54)
2 tablespoons mirin
1 teaspoon sugar
Pinch of salt

1 Soak the freeze-dried tofu in lukewarm water, holding it down with a weight, so that it becomes saturated with water and softened to the core. Press each piece between both hands to squeeze out the water, then soak again in fresh water and squeeze again. Repeat 3 to 4 times.
2 Combine the sauce ingredients in a pan over medium heat. When it comes to a boil, add the tofu. Cut a piece of aluminum foil or kitchen parchment paper smaller than the diameter of the pan and place directly on top of the contents. Simmer over medium-low heat for about 10 minutes. Add the soy sauce and simmer for an additional 2 minutes.
3 Arrange in serving bowls with the blanched snow peas.

Black Sesame Green Beans

It can be a little tricky to coat green beans with sesame seeds, but it goes better if you make the batter rather stiff. This is an unusual way to enjoy the delicious pairing of sesame and green beans.

Serves 2

10 green beans
4 tablespoons flour
2–3 tablespoons water
3 tablespoons black sesame seeds
Vegetable oil, for frying
Salt, to taste

1 Remove the ends from the green beans. Put the flour in a bowl and dip the beans in so that they are thoroughly dusted with flour. Set the beans aside. Mix the water into the remaining flour 1 tablespoon at a time, stopping when you have a fairly stiff batter. Coat the green beans with the batter, then roll them in the sesame seeds to coat thickly.
2 Heat about ½ inch (1 cm) of oil in a skillet to 340°F (170°C) over medium heat. Add the coated green beans and fry until crisp. Drain well on paper towels and sprinkle with salt before serving.

Simmered Turnips with Tofu

Turnips taste better if they retain some texture, so turn off the heat before they get too soft. It's also important to select turnips that are tender rather than fibrous.

Serves 2

2 small Asian or baby turnips
1 piece deep-fried tofu (abura-age)
2 tablespoons light soy sauce

FOR THE SIMMERING SAUCE

1½ cups (360 ml) dashi stock (see page 54)
1 tablespoon sake
1 tablespoon mirin

1 Cut off most of the turnip greens, leaving about a finger's width at the crown. Peel the turnips thickly and cut each one into 6 to 8 wedges. Cut the deep-fried tofu into thin strips.

2 Combine all the simmering sauce ingredients in a pan over medium heat and add the turnips. When it comes to a boil, add the soy sauce. Cut a piece of aluminum foil or kitchen parchment paper smaller than the diameter of the pan and place directly on top of the contents. Simmer for 2 to 3 minutes over low heat. Remove from the heat and test turnips with a skewer or toothpick. Leave them to keep cooking in residual heat if they are still too firm, or take them out if they are soft enough.

Chicken Noshiyaki

This is an everyday variation of the *matsukaze yaki* chicken loaf that my mother makes every year for *osechi*, the New Year's feast. It is juicy and flavorful, with aonori seaweed powder and poppy seeds as accents. This will keep in the refrigerator for 2 to 3 days.

Serves 2

8 oz (250 g) ground chicken
½ teaspoon salt
Aonori seaweed powder, to taste
White poppy seeds or white sesame seeds

FOR THE EGG MIXTURE
1 medium egg
1 tablespoon flour
½ teaspoon sugar
2 teaspoons light soy sauce
2 teaspoons mirin

1 Combine the ground chicken and salt in a bowl and mix well until the meat is sticky. In a separate bowl, whisk all the egg mixture ingredients together. Add to the meat and mix well again. Refrigerate for 30 minutes.
2 Lay out two sheets of aluminum foil and divide the mixture between the two. Spread out to make 2 x 3 inch (5 x 8 cm) rectangles.
3 Broil the mixture on the foil until it's about 80 percent cooked. Take it out and flip it over and cover the surface with aonori seaweed powder and poppy seeds. Return to the broiler and keep cooking until lightly browned.
4 Rest for about a minute so that the juices settle, and cut into bite-sized pieces to serve.

Pea Shoots with Squid Liver

Squid liver has a very rich umami flavor, so the only additional seasonings needed are sake and salt. I love the combination of soft spear squid with the fresh green taste of pea shoots.

Serves 2

1 fresh squid (preferably spear squid), about 10 oz (300 g) total
10 oz (300g) pea shoots
1 tablespoon vegetable oil
¾ inch (2 cm) length ginger, finely slivered
2 tablespoons sake
¼ teaspoon salt

1 Pull the legs off the squid, along with the entrails. Remove the quill from the body of the squid and rinse the body well. Cut into ½ inch (1 cm) wide strips. Remove the eyes and hard beak and cut the legs into pieces. Remove and discard the ink sac. Roughly chop the gastric sac, which contains the liver.
2 Cut the roots off the pea shoots and slice the shoots into thirds. Heat the oil in a skillet over medium heat and stir-fry the ginger until fragrant. Add the cut squid and its liver, turn the heat to high, and stir-fry until the squid turns white. Add the sake and the salt.
3 Add the pea shoots and stir-fry quickly, mixing everything together.

Broiled Salmon in Dashi Sauce

Salmon is quite light in flavor and umami, so here it is doused in a dashi-stock-based sauce. The broiled shishito peppers add a tasty accent. This keeps in the refrigerator for 3 to 4 days.

Serves 2

2 pieces fresh salmon, about 3 oz (90 g) each
Salt
4 shishito peppers or other mildly spicy peppers, for garnish

FOR THE SAUCE
5 tablespoons dashi stock (see page 54)
2 tablespoons soy sauce
2 teaspoons sake
2 teaspoons mirin

1 Lightly salt both sides of the salmon and let stand for 15 minutes. Pat dry.
2 Combine all the sauce ingredients in a small pan and bring to a boil. Transfer to a container wide enough to hold the salmon.
3 Broil or grill the salmon on both sides. Add to the container with the sauce and refrigerate for half a day to a whole day, turning occasionally.
4 Let the salmon come back to room temperature before serving. Serve with the broiled shishito peppers.

Seven-Color Squash

This is a traditional Buddhist vegan dish that our family serve as an offering to our ancestors in Nara, where my mother is from. Kabocha squash is used as a coating sauce, which really brings out the sweetness of the vegetables. Any leftovers will keep in the refrigerator for about 2 days.

Serves 2

1 dried shiitake mushroom
1 teaspoon soy sauce
⅛ kabocha squash, about 5 oz (150 g), seeds and pith removed
1 taro root
½ teaspoon salt
2 green beans
4 inch (10 cm) length burdock root
1 small Japanese or Asian eggplant
1 myoga ginger bud or young ginger shoot
1 piece deep-fried tofu (abura-age)

FOR THE MISO-SESAME SAUCE
2 tablespoons miso
1½ tablespoons sugar
2 tablespoons ground sesame seeds

1 Soak the shiitake mushroom in water until soft. Remove and discard the stem and slice the cap thinly. Put the shiitake mushroom in a small pan and add enough of its soaking water to cover. Add the soy sauce and simmer for 5 minutes. Remove from the heat and let stand until cool.

2 Cut the kabocha squash into 4 to 6 pieces. Peel the taro root and cut into 6 pieces. Slice the eggplant into ¼ inch (5 mm) rounds. Shave the burdock root as if you were sharpening a pencil and soak in water. Remove the ends from the green beans.

3 Put the kabocha squash and taro root in a pan. Cover amply with water and place over medium heat. Cook until tender, then remove. Add the ½ teaspoon of salt to the same pan. Add the green beans and cook until tender, then remove, then cook the burdock root and finally the eggplant. (Be sure to cook the eggplant last so the other vegetables do not get discolored.)

4 Thinly slice the cooked green beans diagonally. Slice the myoga ginger into thin rounds and put into a bowl of water, then drain. Blanch the deep-fried tofu in boiling water to remove the surface oil, then cut into thin strips.

5 Put the kabocha squash in a bowl and mash coarsely. Combine the miso-sesame sauce ingredients, add to the bowl, and stir well to blend. Add the drained shiitake, taro root, burdock root, eggplant, green beans and deep-fried tofu and mix lightly. Allow to sit until a little moisture comes out of the vegetables, then serve.

Shuko Takigiya

Classic Japanese Small Bites

Shuko Takigiya is located in Araki-cho in Shinjuku, an area packed with drinking spots. They serve traditional Japanese drinking accompaniments without ever straying from their vision. In addition to the excellent food, the *junmai* sake varieties recommended by the owner are worth a visit all on their own.

Make standard dishes with basic seasonings

The cooking at my establishment is based on the question, "What does it mean to be standard?" We cook standard dishes, keeping to the basics, following standard methods. The reason for this is that Shuko Takigiya is an izakaya where only *junmai-shu*—that is, sake made just with rice, *koji* mold and water—is served. Accordingly, we aim for a place where dishes are made without the addition of any umami seasonings. The seasonings we use are just the basics: soy sauce, mirin, sake and vinegar. Furthermore, we only use "real" ingredients that contain no MSG or other additives. Selecting high-quality ingredients is also important. For instance, a cucumber that doesn't taste good to begin with can't be improved even by adding the best-tasting vinegar dressing. So we are very particular about the ingredients we choose.

Observe well with the eyes and taste well with the tongue

The keys to improving your cooking technique are controlling the heat and tasting as you go. If a dish doesn't look the way it's supposed to, even though you followed the recipe, in most cases the heat is the problem. For example, even if the recipe says to cook taro root over medium heat for 20 minutes, "medium heat" is interpreted differently by different people, and the taro root itself varies depending on

Tips from Chef Kobayashi of Shuko Takigiya

1. Taste frequently and attentively

Taste throughout the cooking process, to check flavors and textures. It's important to follow a recipe, but in the end the food should taste the way you want it to.

2. Observe the food carefully as it cooks

Check what you are cooking frequently as it is on the heat, both by sight and by feel. The ingredients mustn't be too tough or too soft. Exploring the limit between the two is a way to really push your cooking forward.

3. Use my dashi stock recipe

My recipe makes an all-purpose dashi combining the best features of *ichiban* (first) dashi with those of *niban* (second) dashi (made using the leftovers of ichiban dashi). The key is to keep the temperature under 175°F (80°C) as the kombu simmers. Once the dashi is done, confirm that it has a full, pleasant flavor by taking a sip or two.

the season. Sometimes it will still be hard even after 40 minutes of cooking. In that case, it's important to test it by piercing it with a skewer or toothpick to determine for yourself whether it's cooked through properly. These kinds of observations are essential to good cooking.

Tasting is the same thing—in fact, it's simply observing with your taste buds. For example, a simmered dish will become more concentrated as it is cooked, so you need to taste it at the point where you add the seasonings, and then taste it again when it has finished cooking. This way you can gauge how the flavors change from the point where you add the seasonings to when the dish is done.

The cooking at Shuko Takigiya is nothing unusual. The only noteworthy point is that I always taste everything very diligently, and I believe that leads to good results. Anyone can taste a dish—but you have to know how to taste properly while following a recipe. This is how you can really understand what's in a recipe, including what may have been left out of your cookbook.

Among the recipes I share with you in this book, I have included a recipe for making dashi stock (see page 54), but this is not the standard *ichiban dashi* or "first dashi" that is made with fresh, new, base ingredients. Ichiban dashi was originally intended for use at high-end establishments, where it is usually made on the spot as the orders come in to the kitchen. But in home cooking, dashi is mostly used to make *nimono* or simmered dishes, so it doesn't have to be so fussy. The dashi recipe that I have given instructions for here is simmered lightly after the bonito flakes are added. It retains the fragrance of the bonito flakes while also adding the richness of flavor that's a feature of *niban dashi* or "second dashi." I hope you give this versatile stock a try.

Simmered Taro Root

Making sure the taro roots are not too firm, but not too soft, is essential to this dish. The technique of adding additional bonito flakes (called *katsuobushi* in Japanese) to a simple dashi-based simmered dish like this one is called *oi-gatsuo*, or "adding katsuo." This makes enough for leftovers, which will keep in the refrigerator for about 3 days.

Serves 2

6 taro roots
6 snow peas, for garnish

FOR THE SIMMERING SAUCE
2 cups (450 ml) All-Purpose Dashi Stock (see recipe below)
1 tablespoon light soy sauce
½ tablespoon sake
½ teaspoon salt
½ cup (5 g) bonito flakes, plus extra for garnish
2 x 4 inch (5 x 10 cm) piece kombu seaweed

1 Remove the tops and bottoms of the taro roots. Peel and cut into a hexagonal shape. Rinse briefly with cold water.
2 Bring an ample amount of water to a boil in a pot and add the taro roots. Reduce to a gentle boil and cook for about 20 minutes, or until a bamboo skewer or toothpick goes through one easily, stirring occasionally so that they don't get stuck to the bottom of the pan. Meanwhile, blanch the snow peas in salted water until just tender. Drain the snow peas and taro roots and allow to cool.
3 Combine all the simmering sauce ingredients in a pan over medium heat. (To eliminate the need to strain the sauce later, you can put the bonito flakes in a large tea bag.) When the sauce comes to a boil, turn off the heat. Remove the kombu and the teabag containing the bonito flakes, or strain the liquid.
4 Add the parboiled taro roots to the simmering sauce. Place over medium-low heat and simmer gently for about 20 minutes, then turn off the heat. Cover the pan with a paper towel and let stand until cool.
5 Transfer to a serving plate. Serve topped with the blanched snow peas and the additional bonito flakes.

All-Purpose Dashi Stock

This flavorful stock combines the best features of traditional *ichiban dashi* or "first dashi" and *niban dashi* or "second dashi." It can be used in a wide variety of foods, from clear soups to simmered dishes.

Serves 4

4 cups (1 liter) water
2 pieces kombu seaweed, each about 4 x 4 inches (10 x 10) cm
3 cups (30 g) bonito flakes

Put 8½ cups (2 liters) water in a pot. Put in two pieces of kombu seaweed, each about 4 x 4 inch (10 x 10 cm), and leave to soak overnight. In the morning, set the pot over medium heat and bring to a bare simmer. Remove the kombu as soon as the dashi reaches 175°F (80°C) (if it reaches a higher temperature, the liquid will become cloudy). Turn off the heat and add 6 cups (60 g) bonito flakes. When the bonito flakes sink to the bottom, return the pan to medium heat. When it begins to come to a boil, turn off the heat. Strain the dashi slowly through a sieve lined with paper towels.

Tomatoes Marinated in Tosa Vinegar

The key to this dish is the mild, flavorful vinegar dressing, which takes its name from an ancient province of Japan. Start this dish a day in advance. If you have leftovers, the marinated tomatoes will keep in the refrigerator for 3 to 4 days.

Serves 2

2 to 3 ripe tomatoes
2 inch (5 cm) strip kombu seaweed

FOR THE TOSA VINEGAR DRESSING
1¼ cups dashi stock (see page 54)
¼ cup soy sauce
¼ cup mirin
¼ cup rice vinegar

1 Combine the Tosa vinegar dressing ingredients.
2 Remove the calyxes from the tomatoes. Put sufficient water to cover the tomatoes in a saucepan. Bring to a boil, then add the tomatoes. When the skins split, remove the tomatoes and plunge into cold water. Drain, remove the skins and pat dry. Place the tomatoes and the kombu in a storage container and pour the Tosa vinegar dressing over to cover. Refrigerate overnight.
3 Arrange the tomatoes in bowls and ladle the dressing over. This is also delicious with cucumbers in sesame Tosa dressing (see below).

Tosa Vinegar Variations

Tosa vinegar dressing will keep for 3 to 4 days. You can add some coarsely ground white sesame seeds to make sesame Tosa dressing. Try using this variation to marinate thinly sliced cucumber that's been sprinkled with salt and squeezed out, along with some thinly sliced myoga ginger buds. Thinly sliced celery sprinkled with salt and squeezed out, then marinated in either of these dressings is also delicious.

Root Vegetable Peel Kinpira

Kinpira—a spicy dish created by stir-frying and simmering—is enormously versatile. You can make it with leftover vegetables, or even with peelings that might usually be discarded. Leftovers will keep in the refrigerator for about 3 days.

Serves 2

10 oz (300 g) daikon radish peelings
2 oz (60 g) carrot peelings
2 teaspoons dark sesame oil
1 red chili pepper, stem and seeds removed
2 tablespoons sake
2 tablespoons mirin
1 scant tablespoon sugar
2 tablespoons soy sauce
Toasted sesame seeds, for garnish

1 Spread out the daikon radish and carrot peelings on a flat sieve and leave to dry for half a day. Cut the peel into thin strips.
2 Heat the sesame oil and chili pepper in a pan until fragrant. Add the daikon and carrot peelings and stir-fry.
3 When the peels become tender, add the sake, mirin, sugar and soy sauce, in that order, and continue to stir-fry until there is almost no moisture left in the pan.
4 Arrange the kinpira on a serving plate and scatter the toasted sesame seeds over, crushing some of them between your fingers.

Lotus and Burdock Root Kinpira

The balance between the sugar and the soy sauce is the key to this dish. If you want to add more soy sauce, be sure to add more sugar, too. These root vegetables, more common in Asia than in the West, are both healthy and delicious.

Serves 2

9 oz (250 g) lotus root
2 teaspoons rice vinegar, divided
½ burdock root, about 2 oz (60 g)
⅓ medium carrot
2 teaspoons dark sesame oil
1 red chili pepper, stem and seeds removed
2 tablespoons sake
2 tablespoons mirin
1 scant tablespoon sugar
2 tablespoons soy sauce
Toasted sesame seeds, for garnish

1 Peel the lotus root and slice thinly; if the root is very large, cut it in half lengthwise first. Put the sliced lotus root in a bowl of water and add 1 teaspoon of the vinegar. Shave the burdock root as if you were sharpening a pencil, and put into another bowl of water with the rest of the vinegar. Cut the carrot into thin matchsticks.
2 Heat the sesame oil and chili pepper in a pan until fragrant. Add the drained lotus and burdock root and stir-fry until tender.
3 Add the sake, mirin, sugar and soy sauce in that order. Continue to stir-fry until the pan is almost dry.
4 Arrange the kinpira on a serving plate and scatter the toasted sesame seeds over, crushing some of them between your fingers.

Celery Kinpira

Kinpira is most commonly made with burdock root or carrots. Here I have used celery, and a neutral oil to bring out the celery's full flavor. I use light soy sauce instead of the usual dark soy sauce, and the only sweetness added is mirin. Servings are best kept small, but any leftovers can be refrigerated for about 2 days.

Serves 2

10 oz (300 g) celery hearts
⅓ medium carrot
1 teaspoon vegetable oil
2 tablespoons sake
2 tablespoons mirin
1 tablespoon light soy sauce

1 Cut the celery hearts into thin slices on the diagonal. Cut the carrot into thin matchsticks.
2 Heat the oil in a skillet over medium heat, turning the pan to coat the surface. Add the celery and carrot and stir-fry until just tender.
3 Add the sake, mirin and soy sauce in that order. Continue cooking until there is almost no moisture left in the pan, then serve.

ABOVE **Lotus and Burdock Root Kinpira;** TOP RIGHT **Celery Kinpira;** BOTTOM RIGHT **Root Vegetable Peel Kinpira**

ABOVE **Vinegar-Marinated Sardine**
LEFT **Vinegar-Marinated Fish (shad)**
BELOW **Vinegar-Marinated Mackerel**

Vinegar-Marinated Sardine

The steps of this recipe are simple, but the results will differ depending on how long you leave the fish in salt and vinegar. Make it several times so that you can really get a feel for the tastes and textures that result from longer or shorter salting and marinating.

Serves 2

1 sardine, filleted, about 3½ oz (100 g) total
Salt, for sprinkling
2 x 2 inch (5 x 5 cm) square kombu seaweed
½ cup (120 ml) rice vinegar

FOR THE GARNISH

Thinly sliced green onion, grated ginger, red water-pepper leaves (benitade) or finely slivered red chili pepper

1 Salt and rinse the sardine as for Vinegar-Marinated Fish on page 61. Put the kombu seaweed on the bottom of a container and lay the fish on top. Add the rice vinegar and marinate for about 5 minutes, then drain.

2 Peel the skin from the sardine, then slice crosswise and form into leaf shapes as for the Vinegar-Marinated Fish (page

62), omitting the shiso and pickled ginger. Arrange on a serving plate with the garnishes.

Vinegar-Marinated Mackerel

Mackerel goes off fast, so use the absolute freshest fish that you can find. Salt it very well, and if the fish is fatty, allow it to stand for a longer time after salting. The marinated mackerel can be stored in the refrigerator for about 2 days. Wrap it in paper towels and cling film after Step 2 and store in a closed container.

Serves 2

1 mackerel, filleted, about 3½ oz (100 g) total
Salt, for sprinkling
2 x 2 inch (5 x 5 cm) square kombu seaweed
½ cup (120 ml) rice vinegar

FOR THE GARNISH

sudachi citrus or lime, grated wasabi, red water-pepper leaves (benitade) or red chili pepper

1 Generously sprinkle a shallow tray or plate with salt and place the mackerel on it, skin-side down. Sprinkle the top side with enough salt to completely cover the fish and leave for about 1 hour (or an hour and 30 minutes if the mackerel is fatty).

2 Rinse the salt off the fish completely and pat dry. Put the kombu seaweed in a container and lay the fish on top. Add the rice vinegar and marinate for about 30 minutes (45 minutes if the mackerel is fatty). Drain off the excess moisture.

3 Place the fish on a flat surface and remove the skin. Make a shallow cut down the length of each fillet, then cut crosswise into ⅓ inch (1 cm) wide pieces. Arrange on a serving plate with the garnishes.

Vinegar-Marinated Fish

Sujime, or vinegar marinating, is a technique used on blue-backed fish such as sardines, shad and mackerel. The fish can be kept in the refrigerator for 2 to 3 days after marinating. Wrap it in paper towels and cling film after Step 2 and store in a closed container.

Serves 2

2 fresh blue-backed fish (sardines, shad or mackerel), cleaned, boned and butterflied, about 3½ oz (100 g) total)
Salt, for sprinkling
2 x 2 inch (5 x 5 cm) square kombu seaweed
½ cup (120 ml) rice vinegar

FOR SERVING

Green shiso leaves, pickled sushi ginger, grated wasabi, red water-pepper leaves (benitade) or finely slivered red chili pepper

1 Sprinkle a shallow tray or plate with salt and place the fish on it skin-side down. Sprinkle the top side with more salt and leave for about 30 minutes.

2 Rinse the salt off the fish completely and pat the fish dry. Put the kombu seaweed on the bottom of a container and lay the fish on top. Add the rice vinegar and marinate for about 15 minutes (or about half the time it was rested after salting), then drain.

3 To create the leaf shape for serving, cut each fish in half lengthwise. Lay two pieces on a flat surface skin-side down. Place a green shiso leaf and a slice of pickled sushi ginger on top of each piece, and top with the remaining piece turned skin-side up, as shown in (a) below. Cut crosswise into 6 pieces (b) then line the pieces up so that you have 3 pairs of cut fish (c). Turn the pieces over so the cut sides are facing up (d) and arrange carefully on a plate, pushing them together to prevent the layers from falling apart. Place the red water-pepper leaves or slivered red pepper alongside.

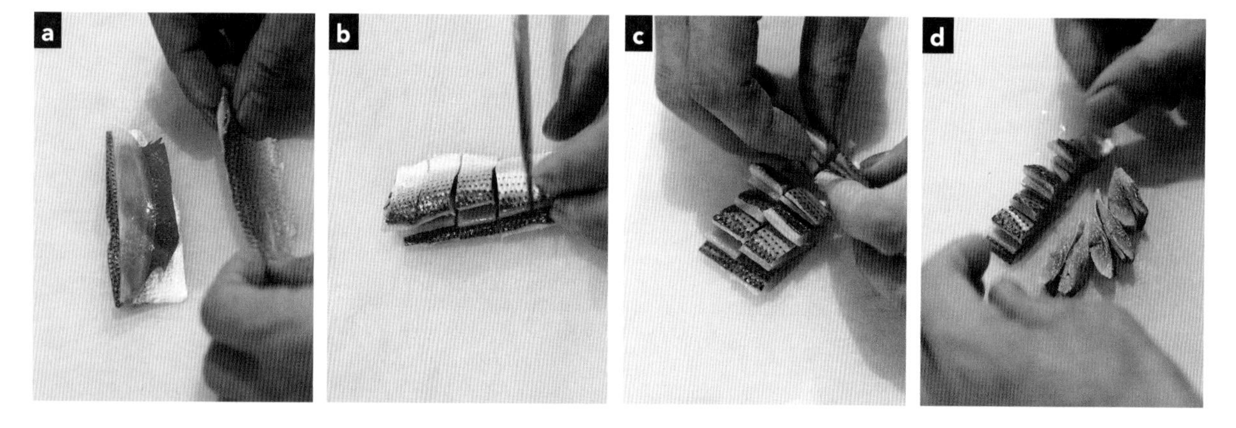

Grated Yam with Miso

This is a take on a traditional dish that uses a mountain yam called Yamato-imo. If you can't find it, you can use *nagaimo* or Chinese yam instead. Be sure to take the time to grind or process the yam until it's very smooth. The dish has a viscous consistency—a texture much loved in Japan!—and is slurped from the bowl. Leftovers will keep, refrigerated, for 2 days.

Serves 2

1⅔ cups (400 ml) dashi stock (see page 54)
2 tablespoons white miso
1 piece Yamato-imo, nagaimo or Chinese yam, about 3½ oz (100 g)

1 Bring the dashi to a boil in a pan over medium heat. When it is bubbling slightly, turn off the heat. Dissolve the white miso in the dashi and allow to cool. Refrigerate until completely chilled.

2 Peel the yam and grate it. Transfer the grated yam to a mortar. Use a pestle to grind and stir the yam about 100 times until it is completely smooth. (A food processor may be used if you don't have a mortar.)

3 Add the dashi-miso mixture to the ground yam a little at a time, continually stirring and grinding to make a very smooth mixture.

Green Onions in Nuta Sauce

Nuta sauce is a traditional miso and vinegar based dressing; this variation uses Egg Miso (see facing page) in place of regular miso. Instead of the very thin green onions used here, try mixing this sauce with slightly bitter green vegetables or herbs, wakame seaweed, fresh shellfish, or vinegar-marinated fish.

Serves 2

2½ cups (600 ml) water
3 teaspoons salt
1 bunch very thin green onions, about 4 oz (120 g) total
Toasted sesame seeds, for garnish
Red water-pepper leaves(benitade) or finely slivered red chili pepper, for garnish

FOR THE NUTA SAUCE
1 oz (30 g) egg miso (see recipe on facing page)
2 teaspoons rice vinegar
1 teaspoon karashi mustard or English mustard

1 Combine all the nuta sauce ingredients in a bowl and mix well until smooth.

2 Bring the water to a boil in a pan and add the salt. Briefly blanch the green onions then transfer them briefly to a bowl of ice water to fix the bright green color. Drain well. Place the onions on a cutting board and scrape along their length several times with the back of a knife to remove any sliminess.

3 Cut the onions into bite-sized pieces and mix with the sauce. Arrange on a serving plate. Sprinkle with sesame seeds and top with red water-pepper leaves or slivered red chili pepper.

Egg Miso

This easy-to-make amount will keep in the refrigerator for about 2 weeks.

Makes about ½ cup (300 g)

¾ cup (200 g) miso
1 egg yolk
4 tablespoons sugar
1 teaspoon sake

1 Combine all the ingredients in a bowl.
2 In a pan large enough for the bowl to fit over, bring water to a boil, then reduce the heat to very low. Place the bowl of combined ingredients over the pan so the bottom is touches the water. Stir continuously with a rubber spatula as the mixture cooks.
3 When the egg miso is thick enough that the spatula leaves a path as it scrapes across the bottom of the bowl, remove from the heat and allow to cool.

Using Egg Miso

Egg miso is a very versatile sauce to have on hand. You can use it to make various nuta dishes as shown here, or spread it on drained tofu or konnyaku slices and grill them to make a classic dish called *dengaku*. The egg miso recipe given here is quite sweet; you can reduce the sugar by half if you prefer. Try spreading it on deep-fried eggplant slices and broiling (see photo at right), or use it as a dipping sauce for fish, meat or vegetables.

Asparagus Nuta

Peel the root ends of the asparagus spears. Blanch the spears in salted water until just tender, then transfer to a bowl of ice water to fix the green color. Drain and cut into diagonal slices. Mix with nuta sauce as in the Green Onions in Nuta Sauce (facing page). Sprinkle with toasted sesame seeds to serve. See photo at right, top.

"Thunder-Dried" Winter Melon Nuta

Cut the top and bottom from a winter melon and scoop out the seeds. Slide a knife around the melon in a spiral pattern, with the spirals about ⅔ inch (1.5 cm) apart, cutting only to the center of the melon. Submerge in a 3 percent salt-water solution for 30 minutes, then drain well. Carefully pull the spiral open and allow to dry for about 8 hours. (If you can't manage to make a spiral, you can just slice the winter melon and dry the slices instead.) Cut the spiral into bite-sized pieces. Mix 1 ounce (30 g) of the dried winter melon with the nuta sauce from the Green Onions in Nuta Sauce (facing page). Sprinkle with toasted sesame seeds to serve. See photo at right, bottom.

Semi-Dried Sea Eel

Rinse the sea eel (*anago* in Japanese) well first, to remove any sliminess. This can be made about 2 days ahead: dry it well and wrap in cling film after Step 2, then refrigerate.

Serves 2

1 sea eel (anago), filleted
2½ cups (600 ml) water
5 teaspoons salt
2 inch (5 cm) square dried kombu seaweed
Grated wasabi, salt, sudachi citrus or lime, for garnish

1 Wipe the sliminess off the surface of the sea eel with a paper towel. Mix the salt and water to make a solution and submerge the kombu and eel in it. Let stand for 30 minutes.
2 Rinse the eel well. Hang on a line (use clips or pegs) in a well-ventilated place out of direct sunlight. Allow to dry for half a day.
3 Grill skin-side up on a preheated grill until the eel is about 80 percent cooked. Finish by briefly grilling the skin side over direct heat until it browns and becomes fragrant. Slice thinly and serve with grated wasabi, salt and sudachi or lime slices.

Semi-Dried Mackerel

The time needed to dry the fish varies, so keep an eye on it and let it continue to dry until it reaches the consistency you want. This can be made about 2 days ahead: dry it well and wrap in cling film after Step 2, then refrigerate.

Serves 2

2 mackerel or other small oily fish, filleted
2½ cups (600 ml) water
5 teaspoons salt
2 inch (5 cm) square dried kombu seaweed
Grated daikon radish, soy sauce, sudachi citrus, for garnish

1 Remove the stomach-side bone and the tough bony part on the side of the fish.
2 Mix the water and salt to make a solution. Submerge the kombu seaweed and mackerel for 30 minutes. (If the fish is pink in color and quite oily, allow it to soak for 5 minutes longer.) Rinse briefly, pat dry and hang in a well-ventilated place out of the sun for half a day.
3 Cut crosshatched slits in the skin (photo a). Roll up each fillet with the skin side facing outward and thread on two metal skewers. Cook on a preheated grill until browned and crisp on the outside (photo b).
4 Remove the skewers. Serve with grated daikon radish drizzled with soy sauce and a slice of sudachi citrus or lime.

a

b

TOP **Semi-Dried Sea Eel**
BOTTOM **Semi-Dried Mackerel**

Simple Soybeans

In Japanese I call this dish "Miso Mame," though it contains no miso. It's a play on words: soybeans, the main ingredient in miso, are called *miso mame*; "Miso Mame" is also the name of one of my favorite *rakugo* (traditional comedy) routines.

Serves 2

3⅓ oz (100 g) large soybeans, dried
1 large green onion or thin leek, green and white parts, thinly sliced
Karashi mustard or English mustard, to taste
Soy sauce, to taste

1 Rinse and drain the soybeans. Soak overnight in ample water.
2 Place a steamer basket over boiling water. Drain the beans and add them to the steamer. Cover and steam for an hour or more, until beans are soft.
3 Spoon into individual serving bowls and top with the green onion. Add mustard and soy sauce to taste. Stir well before eating.

Sake-Simmered Whelks

This is not hard to make as long as you keep an eye on the cooking heat. If you let the simmering liquid boil, the whelks will become tough, so be sure to simmer slowly at a low heat. Leftovers will keep in the refrigerator for about 3 days.

Serves 3

1 lb (500 g) whelks, in shell
1¼ cups (300 ml) water
4 inch (10 cm) length kombu seaweed
1¼ cups (300 ml) sake
1 tablespoon soy sauce, or to taste

1 Wash the whelks in water, rubbing the shells against each other to clean them. Put the whelks in a pan with ample water and set over medium heat. Remove the whelks just before the water comes to a boil. Plunge into cold water, then drain well.
2 Combine the 1¼ cups (300 ml) water, the kombu seaweed and the sake in a pan. Add the parboiled whelks and set over medium heat. Just before the pan comes to a boil, turn the heat down to low and simmer for 20 to 30 minutes, occasionally removing any scum. Do not allow to boil.
3 Remove from the heat and add soy sauce to the pan to taste (the amount depends on how salty the whelks are to begin with). Allow to cool so that the whelks absorb the flavors.

Shutei Zorome

Unique Drinking Food with a Twist

Shutei Zorome is in the Monzen-Nakacho district of Tokyo, which has a real old-fashioned downtown vibe. There's just a counter here, conveying the atmosphere of a simple bar, so the carefully prepared, satisfying small-plate dishes are a surprise.

Recreate flavors from your travels

My place brings together great food that I've sampled in various places around the country. Whenever I eat something tasty, I want to try to make it myself. And then I want everyone else to eat it, so I put it on my menu. In other words, my cooking can be defined as "great food that I had somewhere else." I want to make something because it really impressed me, and I think about how I can recreate it. For me, the pathway to a goal is not important; as long as I can achieve flavors that are close to what I remember, that's enough. So at home I use instant dashi stock granules a lot. To be honest, they are very high quality. If you do a side-by-side comparison of dashi made with granules to dashi made from scratch, there's barely any difference. It's a lot of work to make dashi stock from scratch every day, right? You need to eat every day, and you can't be working so hard all the time. As long as the flavors are the same, I don't think you need to worry about using shortcuts.

When I am trying to recreate flavors, I'm always making calculations. If something is too salty after I make it once, I'll try it again with half the amount of soy sauce. So I'm converting the delight I felt when I first tried the dish into concrete numbers that will allow me to make the dish successfully myself. It's quite hard! But I do think it's important to measure properly when you are following a recipe from a book. If the results aren't to your taste, you just have to change the amounts accordingly.

Group similar tasks together

In order to improve as a cook, pay attention to your process. When you are making two or three items at once, think about the steps you should follow for maximum efficiency. In my case, I start by setting out all the ingredients I'll be using in the amounts I need, and putting away the rest. Taking things out and putting them back uses up a surprising amount of time, and it's tiring too. Next, carry out all the cutting and chopping tasks, then you have left is the heating. Group similar tasks together to reduce your movements.

Once you start heating things, that's the time to wash up. A lot of people just concentrate on the cooking part because they want to finish up fast. But if your kitchen is full of things to wash up when the food is done, it's really disheartening. Cooking is only complete when the washing-up is done, so if you can cook while factoring that in as a step, I think you can call yourself a good cook.

Even when I'm referring to a recipe to make something, I write out the required ingredients and general steps beforehand. I do this on a piece of paper at my desk, sitting down, and I decide on what to change as I'm doing it. By writing things down, I can establish them in my head, so there's no need to keep opening up the cookbook and referring to it. It saves time and makes the cooking process go much more smoothly.

Tips from Chef Ono of Shutei Zorome

1. Use instant dashi stock granules

A lot of people seem to think you always need to make dashi stock from scratch, but I think it's fine to use instant dashi stock granules as long as you know how the stock will taste and use them judiciously. I usually buy the kind without any additives.

2. Prepare all the ingredients in advance

Don't take out the ingredients just before you need them, but have everything laid out and ready beforehand. Cut up what you need and put away the rest. This way your workspace will remain clear, and your cooking will be more efficient.

3. Write down a recipe and edit it in your head

Cooking something haphazardly will always fail. It just takes 10 minutes to sit down and write out a recipe in your own terms before you start. I strongly recommend this practice. Your head and heart will calm down, and you won't feel rushed or panicked while you are cooking.

Soy-Sauce-Marinated Tuna

Blanching the tuna imparts two delightful textures: the cooked surface that is permeated with the marinade and the soft, rich interior. Leftovers will keep in the refrigerator for about 3 days. Wrap the fish well, first with paper towels and then with cling film, so that the cut surfaces of the tuna are not exposed to air.

Serves 2

5 oz (150 g) sashimi-grade tuna
Shredded daikon radish, shredded green shiso leaves, shiso seed pods, water-pepper leaves and grated wasabi, for garnish

FOR THE MARINADE
4 tablespoons soy sauce
2½ tablespoons sake
2 teaspoons mirin

1 Combine all the marinade ingredients in a pan over medium heat and stir well so that the alcohol evaporates. Leave to cool.
2 Fill a small pan halfway with water and bring it to a boil. Turn off the heat, then submerge the tuna in the hot water for 10 seconds. Transfer immediately to a bowl of ice water. When the tuna is cool, drain and carefully wipe off all moisture.
3 Put the tuna and the cooled marinade together in a self-sealing bag. Squeeze out the air and close the bag. Refrigerate for an hour.
4 Slice the marinated tuna into bite-sized pieces and arrange on a serving plate with the garnishes.

Ginger Scallops with Umeboshi Plum Sauce

If you quickly grill the surface of scallops, the nutty fragrance will become an irresistible flavor accent. The sweetness of the scallops and the slight bitterness of the myoga ginger buds are a great match.

Serves 2

4 large scallops
1 myoga ginger bud, or a little red onion
½ inch (1 cm) length ginger, finely slivered
Shiso buds and toasted sesame seeds, for garnish

FOR THE UMEBOSHI SAUCE
1 umeboshi salt-pickled plum
1 green shiso leaf
Large pinch bonito flakes
A little dashi stock (see page 54) to thin the sauce

1 Remove the tough parts of the scallops. Place on a heated grill and cook just until the surface is lightly singed. Cut each scallop into quarters. Shred the myoga ginger finely.
2 To make the umeboshi sauce, pit the umeboshi and chop into a paste with a knife. Finely mince the green shiso leaf. Rub the bonito flakes between your fingers to make a fine powder. Mix all three ingredients together, then thin with a little dashi stock.
3 Toss the scallops with the umeboshi sauce to coat evenly. Arrange on a serving plate and top with the garnishes.

Red Cabbage Coleslaw

Red cabbage tends to be firmer than green, so it's well suited to coleslaw. Soaking the vegetables in a salt-water solution makes them flavorful and tender.

Serves 2

¼ red cabbage, about 10 oz (300 g), shredded
3 tablespoons shredded carrot
¼ medium onion, thinly sliced lengthwise
2 cups (500 ml) water
1 tablespoon salt
Dill, for garnish, optional

FOR THE DRESSING
6 tablespoons mayonnaise
2 tablespoons rice vinegar
1¼ teaspoons sugar
A little coarsely ground black pepper

1 Put the red cabbage, carrot and onion in a bowl. Mix the water and salt together until the salt is dissolved. Pour over the vegetables and let stand for about an hour.
2 Combine all the dressing ingredients in a large bowl.
3 Drain the vegetables and squeeze out the excess moisture. Add to the dressing and mix well. Arrange on a serving plate and top with sprigs of dill, if desired.

Mackerel Tartare with Miso

Minced raw fish mixed with miso is called *namero* in Japanese. There are varying opinions as to how finely to mince the fish; I'm one of those who like it very smooth and paste-like. The miso, the green onion and the ginger cut any fishy flavors.

Serves 2

1 very fresh mackerel, filleted (other small oily fish may be used)
½ oz (15 g) green onion or thin leek
¾ inch (2 cm) length ginger
1 tablespoon red miso
½ sheet toasted nori seaweed, cut into eighths
Green shiso leaves, minced green onion and toasted sesame seeds, for garnish

1 Remove any bones from the fish. Peel off the skin and cut the meat into pieces. Finely mince the green onion and ginger.
2 Combine the fish, ginger and green onions with the miso on a cutting board. Chop and turn the mixture continuously with a knife until it turns into a paste.
3 Arrange on a serving plate accompanied by the nori pieces and garnishes. Spoon some of the tartare onto a piece of nori seaweed to eat.

Crispy Fried Burdock Root

It's remarkable how tender this usually rather tough vegetable can become. Enjoy the contrast between the crisp outside and the soft inside.

Serves 2

3 burdock roots, about 1 lb (450 g) total
1⅔ cups (400 ml) dashi stock (see page 54)
3 tablespoons light soy sauce
3 tablespoons mirin
4 tablespoons water (more if needed)
6 tablespoons all-purpose flour
Vegetable oil, for frying
Salt, pepper, aonori seaweed powder

1 Cut the burdock root into 3 inch (8 cm) pieces. Place in a saucepan with ample water and bring to a boil. Cut a piece of aluminum foil or kitchen parchment paper into a circle smaller than the diameter of the pan. Set directly on the water, lower heat to medium, and cook the burdock root for about an hour, or until a bamboo skewer pierces it easily. Drain well.

2 Combine the dashi stock, light soy sauce and mirin in a pan and bring to a boil. Add the burdock root and bring to a boil. Turn off the heat and let stand until cool so that the burdock root absorbs the flavors.

3 Mix the water and flour together to make a thick paste, adding more water if needed. Coat the seasoned burdock root in the paste. In a heavy pan, heat 2 inches (5 cm) oil to 340ºF (170ºC) oil and deep-fry the battered burdock root until crisp.

4 Drain the fried burdock on paper towels. Sprinkle with salt, pepper and aonori seaweed powder and serve while still hot.

Juicy Chicken with Vegetables

This genius of this simple dish is in the layering of flavors. The juicy texture adds to the pleasure. Fresh okara soybean pulp, a byproduct of tofu and soy milk production, may be found at larger Asian supermarkets. Dried okara may be simmered and drained to reconstitute.

Serves 2

Green part of 1 thin leek or large green onion
⅓ carrot, about ¾ oz (20 g)
4 fresh shiitake mushrooms
2 pieces deep-fried tofu (abura-age)
2 tablespoons dark sesame oil
7 oz (200 g) ground chicken (dark meat)
7 oz (200g) fresh soybean pulp (okara)

FOR THE SIMMERING SAUCE
1⅔ cups (400 ml) dashi stock (see page 54)
3 tablespoons light soy sauce
3 tablespoons mirin
2 tablespoons sugar
1⅓ tablespoons dark soy sauce

1 Finely slice the leek or green onion into thin rounds. Shred the carrot. Cut the stems off the shiitake mushrooms and discard. Slice the shiitake caps thinly. Heat a skillet and lightly toast the deep-fried tofu on both sides, then slice thinly.
2 Heat the sesame oil in a skillet over medium heat. Add the ground chicken and stir-fry. When the meat changes color, add the okara and the vegetables from Step 1 and keep stir-frying. When everything is heated through, add the sauce ingredients and bring to a simmer.
3 When there is almost no liquid left in the pan, but the okara is still moist, turn off the heat.

Sautéed Pork with Whiskey Butter

This is a homage to the sautéed pork served at Sugita, an izakaya in Kuramae, Tokyo. Pair this with hot sake to make the experience complete.

Serves 2

1 slice pork loin, ½ inch (1 cm) thick
Salt and pepper, to taste
Flour, for dusting
1 tablespoon vegetable oil
Karashi mustard or English mustard, to taste
Finely shredded cabbage and coriander leaves, to serve

FOR THE WHISKEY BUTTER
3 tablespoons whiskey
1½ teaspoons soy sauce
2 teaspoons butter
1 teaspoon sugar

1 Make incisions through any sinews in the pork and sprinkle with salt and pepper. Dust with flour, shaking off any excess.
2 Heat the vegetable oil in a skillet. Add the pork and pan-fry over high heat. When it is browned on one side, turn off the heat, flip the pork over and cover the pan with a lid. Leave the pork to cook in the residual heat for 5 minutes. Meanwhile, combine the whiskey butter ingredients.
3 Return the skillet with the pork to the heat and add the combined whiskey butter ingredients. Cook until the alcohol is burned off. (The alcohol might ignite at this point, so be careful.) Take out the pork and reduce the sauce in the pan until thick.
4 Slice the pork into bite-sized pieces and arrange on a plate. Pour the whiskey butter over and put some mustard on the side. Serve with shredded cabbage, fresh coriander leaves, radish sprouts, or other vegetables.

Soybean Chili with Octopus

Chili is generally made with kidney or red beans, but soybeans work well, too. The octopus adds umami and depth of flavor. You can find cooked octopus wherever sashimi is sold.

Serves 2

2 cooked octopus arms
4 slices bacon
½ medium onion
14 oz (400 g) canned whole tomatoes, with the juice
2 tablespoons vegetable oil
1 teaspoon cumin seeds
1 cinnamon stick
5 oz (150 g) mixed ground beef and pork
2 tablespoons tomato ketchup
9 oz (250 g) cooked soybeans
1 slice cheddar cheese
Dill sprigs, for garnish, optional

FOR THE SPICE MIX

1 teaspoon cayenne pepper
1 teaspoon turmeric
1 teaspoon garam masala
1 teaspoon salt

1 Cut the octopus arms into bite-sized pieces. Finely mince the bacon and onion. Crush the canned tomatoes.

2 Heat the vegetable oil in a skillet and add the cumin seeds and cinnamon stick. Stir until fragrant, then add the onion and sauté over medium heat until browned.

3 Add the bacon and ground meat and stir-fry. When the meat has changed color, add the canned tomatoes, ketchup and octopus, and simmer for about 10 minutes. Add the soybeans and simmer for an additional 10 minutes. Combine the spice mix ingredients, add to the skillet and stir. Taste and adjust the seasoning if needed.

4 Pour the chili into an ovenproof dish and lay the cheese on top. Broil on high until the cheese is melted. Top with dill sprigs if desired.

Coriander Gyoza Dumplings

To make these deliciously juicy gyoza dumplings, don't squeeze out the moisture from the napa cabbage as you normally might. The coriander roots lend a refreshing note.

Makes 20 dumplings

FOR THE WRAPPERS

1 cup (160 g) all-purpose flour, plus more for dusting
½ teaspoon salt, dissolved in ⅓ cup (80 ml) water

FOR THE FILLING

⅛ napa cabbage, about 6 oz (180 g)
Small bunch garlic chives, about 1⅔ oz (40 g)
7 oz (200 g) ground pork
1 tablespoon water
½ garlic clove, finely minced
¾ inch (2 cm) length ginger, finely minced
A few fresh coriander roots, about ½ oz (15 g), minced
⅔ teaspoon oyster sauce
1 tablespoon soy sauce
1 teaspoon sugar
1 teaspoon cornstarch
1 teaspoon dark sesame oil
1 teaspoon sake
½ teaspoon salt

TO COOK AND SERVE

3 tablespoons sesame oil, divided
2 tablespoons flour, dissolved in 4 tablespoons water
1 tablespoon soy sauce
1 tablespoon rice vinegar
Karashi or English mustard

1 To make the dumpling wrappers put the flour in a bowl. Add the salt water to the flour in 4 batches, stirring well after each addition. When the dough forms into a ball, knead until smooth. Cover with a damp kitchen towel, then wrap in cling film. Allow to rest at room temperature for 20 minutes.
2 To make the filling, cut the napa cabbage into 1/4 inch (5 mm) pieces. Cut the garlic chives to about the same size. Combine the ground pork and the 1 tablespoon water in a bowl and mix well with your hands until the meat is sticky. Add all the remaining filling ingredients and continue to mix until very sticky. Rest the filling in the refrigerator overnight if time allows.
3 Dust your work surface with flour and divide the dough for the wrappers into 20 pieces. Roll each piece into a 4 inch (10 cm) diameter circle, changing the direction of the rolling pin frequently. Put a tablespoon of the filling on each circle and fold into a crescent shape, pleating the edges if desired.
4 Heat 2 tablespoons of the sesame oil in a skillet over high heat and arrange the gyoza dumplings in a sunburst pattern. Add water to about 1/3 of the height of the dumplings, and cover the pan with a lid to steam-cook them. When there is no moisture left in the pan, add the flour-water mixture. When all the moisture is cooked off again, add the remaining tablespoon of sesame oil to crisp up the lacy "wings" formed by the flour water.
5 Turn the dumplings over onto a plate. Mix the soy sauce and vinegar together to make a dipping sauce. Add a little mustard on the side, if desired.

Simmered Nori with Wasabi

Nori no tsukudani, a savory paste made with nori seaweed, is a staple item in many Japanese households. Combining wasabi with the nori makes this humble side dish into a great drinking accompaniment. This will keep in the refrigerator for about 3 weeks.

Makes about 1 cup
10 sheets dried nori seaweed (see note below)
1/3 cup (90 ml) soy sauce
1/3 cup (90 ml) sake
1/3 cup (90 ml) mirin
2½ tablespoons sugar
Grated fresh wasabi or wasabi paste, to taste

1 Shred the nori into small pieces by hand and soak in water to cover until soft. Drain well.
2 Combine the soy sauce, sake, mirin and sugar in a saucepan and bring to a boil over medium heat. Stir in the nori seaweed and lower the heat. Simmer, stirring constantly, until the mixture softens into a paste.
3 Serve in a mound with wasabi alongside.

NOTE Fresh nori seaweed—that is, nori seaweed that has not been dried—is preferable for this dish, but it is difficult to obtain. If you can find it, use 5 oz (150 g) fresh nori in place of the dried nori sheets in this recipe.

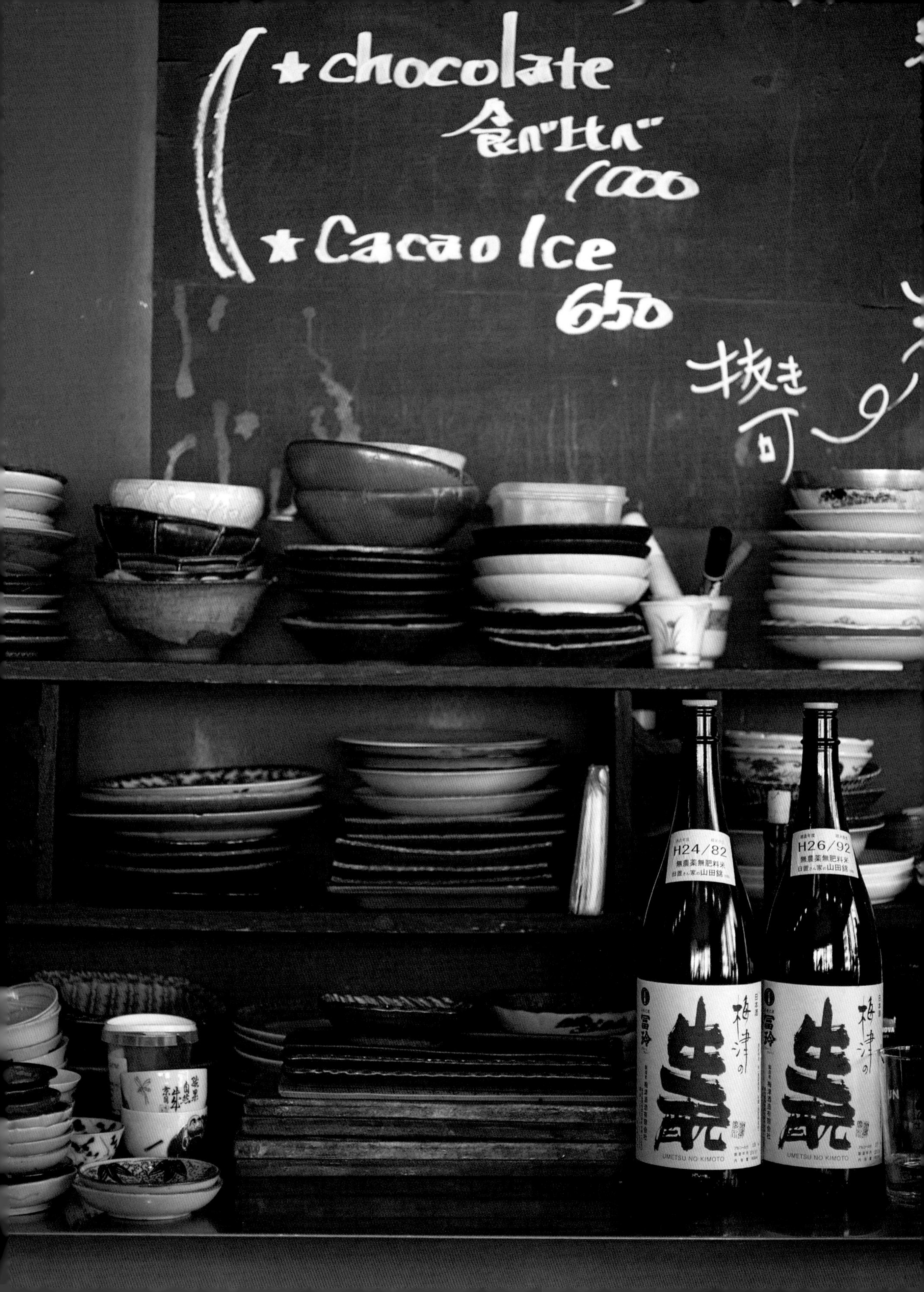

★chocolate
食べ比べ
1000
★Cacao Ice
650
抜き可

H24/82
無農薬無肥料米
日置さん家の山田錦

H26/92
無農薬無肥料米
日置さん家の山田錦

冨玲
梅津の
生酛
UMETSU NO KIMOTO

Sakebozu

Aromatic Multicultural Drinking Accompaniments

Styled like a chic bar, Sakebozu is an unusual izakaya where you can enjoy borderless cuisine incorporating spices and fruit alongside a careful selection of sake offerings.

Try adding spices to your usual cooking

My place serves Japanese sake, but a lot of our cooking uses spices, and we don't have any traditional Japanese dishes on our menu. The thinking behind this is that I want to propose new pairings of sake and food. A lot of people seem to think that they don't know how to use spices properly, and that they can only use them in special dishes, so they end up having a lot left over. But you can add spices to any everyday dish, from simple simmered potatoes and meat or a veggie stir-fry. Just try sprinkling the spices on at the end the way you might add chili pepper or Tabasco. If you add spices in the middle of the cooking process and mix them in, you can't go back, so start out by just adding a little at the very end in this way, and you may encounter some wonderful flavors.

You may think that you need to use a lot of spices at once, as in Indian cooking, but there are lots of dishes where the spices added are much more subtle. Cumin and coriander, for instance, are easy to find, and both have very clean flavors. The first thing I'd recommend you do is to add spices to the salt you sprinkle on deep-fried foods. Oil and spices go very well together, and you'll be able to really taste the spice you add. Don't overthink it—just add the spices the way you might add a dusting of black pepper.

The dishes I serve at my place may seem challenging when you hear their names, but they are just variations of everyday Japanese dishes. Mashed Yam Salad (page 95) is just potato salad, and Steamed Clams and Tomatoes with Thai Fish Sauce (page 101) is a take on the standard Japanese dish of clams steamed with sake. Pork Shabu-Shabu Hot Pot with Spicy Daikon Radish (page 98) is a variation of the regular pork shabu-shabu, but the addition

Tips from Chef Maeda of Sakebozu

1. Add spices to your usual dishes

It's difficult to use spices skillfully from the start. Be more loose and free about spices, and try adding new ones to your usual dishes to find some you like. There are no rules when it comes to using spices.

2. Flavor is determined by how salty a dish is

Whether you think a dish tastes good or not is determined by how salty it is. If it's just right, it tastes good whether it's hot or cold. As you make a dish again and again, you'll become able to gauge what's "just right."

3. Change things to suit your tastes

Use recipes simply as references. Everyone has different tastes, so I think it's a good idea to adjust the flavors to suit the diner. In the process, please find the flavors that you yourself like.

of spices changes the dish into something quite different. This is the fun thing about cooking.

Use cookbooks as a jumping-off point to find the flavors you like

I believe that whether a dish tastes good or not depends on how much salt is added to it. But everyone's tastes differ. Cookbooks should just be used as references. If you try making something from a cookbook and you think it's too sweet or too salty, don't give up at that point—just change things up to suit your tastes. Then you might think, if I'm making a recipe for this person I need to hold back on the seasonings, or I need to season it a bit more heavily for that person—making these kinds of changes is a matter of personal preference, of course. You can change the way you make something to suit different tastes. This is one of the reasons why the dishes we serve at Sakebozu are never really fixed. We adjust the flavors again and again as we continue to develop and improve.

Stir-Fried Chicken with Tofu

This dish is delicious served hot or cold. It's very simple, so try adding some chopped fresh coriander, or sprinkling on some sansho pepper or ground chili pepper.

Serves 2

2 tablespoons light sesame oil or vegetable oil
1½ inch (3 cm) length green onion or thin leek, finely chopped
3½ oz (100 g) ground chicken (dark meat)
½ block silken tofu, about 5 oz (150 g)
6 tablespoons water
½ teaspoon salt
Black pepper
1 teaspoon grated ginger
½ tablespoon rice vinegar

1 Heat the oil in a skillet. Add the chopped green onion or leek and stir-fry until lightly browned.
2 Add the ground chicken and stir-fry while breaking it apart. When the meat is cooked through, break up the tofu with your hands and add it to the pan. Add the water, salt and pepper, and stir to cook off the moisture.
3 When there is almost no moisture left in the pan, taste and add more salt if needed. Stir in the ginger and vinegar to finish.

Wood-Ear Mushrooms and Cucumber in Leek Oil Dressing

When you quickly deep-fry cucumber, some of its moisture will cook out and flavors can penetrate it much more easily. The key to this dish is the fragrant leek oil.

Serves 2

8 to 10 dried wood-ear mushrooms
Water for soaking
2 tablespoons vegetable oil, plus more for deep-frying
1 inch (2.5 cm) piece of leek
1 small Japanese or Asian cucumber

FOR THE DRESSING
1 tablespoon leek oil (see Step 2)
½ tablespoon Thai fish sauce (nam pla)
1 tablespoon rice vinegar
1 teaspoon turmeric powder

1 Reconstitute the wood-ear mushrooms by soaking them in plenty of water until soft.
2 To make the leek oil, heat the 2 tablespoons of vegetable oil to 360°F (180°C). Finely mince the leek and place it in a heatproof bowl, then pour the heated vegetable oil over it.
3 Cut the cucumber in half lengthwise and scoop out the seeds with a spoon. Halve lengthwise again, then cut into 1 to 1½ inch (3 to 4 cm) lengths. In a heavy pan, heat 1 inch (2.5 cm) vegetable oil to 340°F (170°C) and deep-fry the cucumber for about 10 seconds.
4 Drain the softened wood-ear mushrooms well. Whisk all dressing ingredients together and toss with the mushrooms and cucumber.

Tuna with Garlic-Chive Soy Sauce

Marinating strongly scented garlic chives in soy sauce produces a fragrant, well-rounded seasoning. If you have the garlic-chive soy sauce on hand, you can make this dish in minutes.

Serves 2

1¾ oz (50 g) sashimi-grade fresh tuna
1 teaspoon toasted sesame seeds
2 teaspoons olive oil or sesame oil

FOR THE GARLIC-CHIVE SOY SAUCE

Bunch garlic chives, about 3½ oz (100 g), or regular chives plus 1 clove garlic
1 red chili pepper, stem and seeds removed
Soy sauce, to cover

1 To make the garlic-chive soy sauce, cut the garlic chives into 1 inch (2.5 cm) lengths and put into a storage container. Roughly chop the red chili pepper and add. Pour in enough soy sauce to cover. Refrigerate overnight to allow the flavors to infuse the soy sauce.
2 Slice the tuna diagonally into bite-sized pieces.
3 Stir together the sesame seeds, the oil and 1 teaspoon of strained garlic-chive soy sauce in a bowl. Add the tuna and toss to mix. Taste, adding a little more garlic-chive soy sauce if needed.

Homemade garlic-chive soy sauce is great with sashimi, mixed with vegetables, or drizzled on steamed potatoes with a little butter. It's also nice added to a sauce for noodles, or with hot or cold tofu. Leave the garlic chives and red pepper in the soy sauce and refrigerate. It will keep for about 2 weeks.

Spicy Seaweed Stir-Fry

This is based on the traditional Japanese *kinpira*, a spicy stir-fried dish. I've added star anise to it to change it up a bit. If you can obtain fresh wakame seaweed, please give this a try. You can substitute stem wakame (available at Asian grocery stores). However, dried wakame or wakame preserved in salt will not have the right texture for this dish.

Serves 2

2 oz (60 g) fresh wakame seaweed
1 tablespoon sesame oil
1 red chili pepper, stem and seeds removed
1 pod star anise
½ tablespoon finely minced leek or green onion
1 pinch bonito flakes

FOR THE SAUCE
1 teaspoon soy sauce
1 teaspoon mirin
1 teaspoon sake

1 Cut the wakame into bite-sized pieces.
2 Put the sesame oil, red chili pepper and star anise in a skillet over low heat. Cook until fragrant, then turn off the heat and remove the chili pepper and star anise.
3 Put the skillet on high heat, add the wakame and stir-fry quickly. Add the sauce ingredients and stir-fry to evaporate the moisture. Add the leek and bonito flakes and mix quickly.

Mashed Yam Salad

This dish was created when I tried to make potato salad with yam. Mixing the steamed yam with raw sliced yam makes for great texture, and the dried baby sardines add umami and crunch. The salad has a light finish without the heaviness of mayonnaise.

Serves 2

Large piece Chinese yam (nagaimo), about 10 oz (300 g)
Soy sauce or Garlic Chive Soy Sauce (see page 92), to taste
2 myoga ginger buds, thinly sliced (red onion may be substituted)
Toasted white sesame seeds, for garnish

FOR THE DRESSING
1 oz (30 g) dried baby sardines (chirimen-jako)
1 tablespoon olive oil
½ tablespoon rice vinegar

1 Peel two-thirds of the Chinese yam. Place in a steamer and steam for 30 to 35 minutes. Mash while still hot. Combine the dressing ingredients, add to the yam and mix well.

2 Peel the remaining third of the yam, cut in half lengthwise and slice thinly.

3 When the steamed yam is cool, add the sliced raw yam to it and mix. Taste, adding a little soy sauce or Garlic Chive Soy Sauce if needed. Arrange on a serving plate and top with the myoga ginger. Sprinkle toasted sesame seeds on top.

Octopus with Harissa

This is my take on an octopus dish from Galicia in Spain, with a homemade harissa that uses a mild yet fragrant type of Korean chili pepper. You should be able to find cooked octopus wherever sashimi is sold.

SERVES 2

1 leek, white part only
1 cup (240 ml) water
¼ teaspoon salt
2 oz (60 g) cooked octopus
1 small shallot or myoga ginger bud

FOR THE HARISSA

2 tablespoons + 1 teaspoon ground mild Korean chili pepper (gochugaru)
2 tablespoons sweet paprika powder
1 teaspoon ground cumin
1 teaspoon ground coriander
½ tablespoon salt
1 teaspoon sugar
6 tablespoons olive oil

1 To make the harissa, mix all the harissa ingredients together in a glass storage container. Close tightly and refrigerate overnight to let the flavors meld together.

2 Cut the leek into 2 inch (5 cm) pieces. Bring the cup of water to a boil in a pan and add the salt. Boil the leek until tender. Turn off the heat and leave the leek in the water until cooled.

3 Slice the octopus into thin rounds. Slice the shallot or myoga bud thinly diagonally.

4 Add 2 teaspoons of the harissa to the octopus and shallot and mix to coat. Slice the boiled leek in half and serve alongside.

Harissa is a chili-pepper-based paste used in Tunisia and other countries. If covered with cling film to keep it airtight, it will keep at room temperature for three months, so it's worth making it in quantity. Try it on chicken tenders, shrimp, and various vegetables to make instant drinking snacks. You can also use it with various meat dishes as you might use chili paste or chili oil, or add it to noodle soups and sauces or shabu-shabu hot pots.

Pork Shabu-Shabu Hot Pot with Spicy Daikon Radish

This is a spicy take on the classic Japanese shabu-shabu, a kind of hot pot with very thin blanched pork slices served with grated daikon radish and ponzu sauce. I also use Mekabu seaweed, the sprout or blossom at the base of the wakame plant, which can be found in Japanese grocery stores. Be sure to use the "fresh" (reconstituted) kind, not dried.

Serves 2

Small piece daikon radish, about 1 oz (30 g)
¼ teaspoon salt
1 oz (30 g) prepared mekabu seaweed
1 teaspoon soy sauce
2½ oz (70 g) very thinly sliced pork loin
Toasted white sesame seeds, for garnish

FOR THE SPICE MIX
½ teaspoon cumin seeds, crushed
½ teaspoon coriander seeds, crushed
1 to 2 tablespoons lemon juice

1 Grate the daikon radish coarsely. Add the salt and leave for about 15 minutes. Drain off the excess liquid. Combine all the spice mix ingredients and stir into the grated daikon. Mix the mekabu seaweed with the soy sauce.
2 Bring some water to a boil in a pan. Briefly blanch the pork slices. As soon as the meat changes color, remove the pork from the boiling water.
3 Drain the meat well and arrange on serving plates. Top with the spiced daikon radish mix and mekabu seaweed. Sprinkle with sesame seeds before serving.

Marinated Soybeans

This is a standard amuse-bouche at Sakebozu. Instead of being boiled, the soybeans are roasted and then marinated in a spicy soy sauce. This is the kind of bean dish I like: not very sweet (as bean dishes are usually are in Japanese cooking) and full of texture. This will keep in the refrigerator for about 7 days.

Serves 2

7 oz (200 g) dry white or black soybeans

FOR THE MARINADE
1 cup (250 ml) soy sauce
2 cups (500 ml) water
5 tablespoons sugar
1 red chili pepper, stem and seeds removed

1 Soak the soybeans in plenty of water for 6 to 7 hours. Drain into a colander and leave for about 5 hours to dry completely.
2 Combine all the marinade ingredients in a pan and bring to a boil. Turn off the heat.
3 Heat up a skillet and add the soybeans. Roast the soybeans, shaking the skillet constantly, until they are lightly browned.
4 Add the sauce from Step 2 to the skillet and bring to a boil over high heat. Turn off the heat and let stand until cool.

Sour Cream and Olive Dip

I was aiming for a tartar sauce without mayonnaise and tried using sour cream instead. The result was this refined-tasting, tart yet rich dip. It keeps in the refrigerator for about 3 days.

Makes about ⅓ cup (100 g)

¼ medium onion, minced
¼ teaspoon salt
Cold water, for soaking
12 black olives, pits removed
3 tablespoons sour cream
2 teaspoons honey
1 teaspoon soy sauce
A little black pepper
Salt, to taste
Dash coarsely ground pink pepper, optional

1 Sprinkle the minced onion with the salt and massage. Soak in cold water for a few minutes to remove the sharpness, then drain and squeeze out the water. Slice the olives thinly.

2 Mix all the ingredients together, except the pink pepper. Taste, adding a little salt if needed. Arrange on a serving plate and sprinkle with ground pink pepper if desired.

NOTE This is also delicious spread on bread, or served with fried dishes in place of tartar sauce. Try sprinkling a little chopped dill on top.

Steamed Clams and Tomatoes with Thai Fish Sauce

This is our izakaya's take on the classic Japanese dish of sake-steamed clams. With its mix of Southeast Asian and Italian flavors, it feels quite multicultural!

Serves 2

6 oz (180 g) Manila or littleneck clams, sand removed
5 cherry tomatoes
1 oz (35 g) beech mushrooms (shimeji)
⅘ cup (200 ml) water
3 tablespoons sake
⅓ red chili pepper, stem and seeds removed
1 garlic clove, peeled and thinly sliced
½ tablespoon Thai fish sauce (nam pla)
Black pepper
½ tablespoon olive oil
5 to 6 leaves arugula or other slightly bitter green

1 Wash the clams in water, rubbing the shells against each other to clean them. Remove the calyxes from the tomatoes and cut in half lengthwise. Cut the stem ends off the beech mushrooms, and separate the clumps into individual mushrooms.
2 Combine the clams, tomatoes, mushrooms, water, sake, red chili pepper and garlic in a saucepan over medium heat and cover with a lid. Cook for 2 to 3 minutes. As the clams start to open up, remove the ones that have opened.
3 Add the fish sauce and black pepper, adjusting as needed. Drizzle in the olive oil and turn off the heat.
4 Arrange the opened clams and cooked vegetables on a serving plate and top with the arugula.

Shrimp and Turnip with Century-Egg Sauce

The creamy yolk of a century egg is used to make an unctuous, fragrant sauce. Serve it with lightly flavored ingredients to add umami—it will make your drinks taste really good.

Serves 2

⅓ small Asian or baby turnip
1¼ teaspoons salt, divided
1 cup (250 ml) water
6 medium shrimp, shells on
A little cornstarch or potato starch
2 cups (240 ml) water
½ tablespoon Shaoxing wine
1 teaspoon soy sauce
Crushed toasted almonds, for garnish

FOR THE CENTURY-EGG SAUCE
1 century egg
1 teaspoon minced leek or green onion
1 tablespoon dark sesame oil
¾ tablespoon soy sauce
½ tablespoon black vinegar
½ tablespoon Shaoxing wine
Dash cinnamon powder

1 Peel the turnip, cut in half and slice about ¼ inch (5 mm) thick, and place in a self-sealing bag. Dissolve 1 teaspoon of the salt in the water, then add the salt water to the turnips. Squeeze all the air from the bag and seal it. Let stand for about 3 hours.

2 Remove the digestive tracts from the shrimp, keeping the shells on. Rub the shrimp with a little cornstarch to clean them, then rinse under running water. Bring the 2 cups water to a boil, add the remaining ¼ teaspoon salt and then put in the shrimp. When the shrimp change color, turn off the heat and leave them in the water until cool. Peel the shrimp and mix them with the Shaoxing wine and soy sauce.

3 To make the century egg sauce, separated the yolk of the egg from the white; crush the yolk and chop the white roughly. Mix the egg with all the remaining sauce ingredients.

4 Drain the salted turnip very well and arrange on a plate with the shrimp. Pour some century-egg sauce over both and sprinkle toasted almonds on top.

NOTE This recipe makes extra century-egg sauce. Leftover sauce can be served with tofu, boiled vegetables, pork, or roasted bell peppers. It will keep for about 2 days in the refrigerator.

Shaoxing wine, century egg and black vinegar are Chinese ingredients that can be found at a Chinese or general Asian grocery store. I recommend the vacuum-packed century eggs imported from Taiwan if you can find them. They aren't too pungent, and they have a mild flavor and a good texture.

Spicy Pork Belly

Simmered pork belly is a classic Japanese dish. This version is enhanced by a spicy celery chutney. Pork belly is quite high in fat, so the celery is a refreshing complement.

1 lb 2 oz (500 g) pork belly
4 cups (1 liter) water
¾ inch (2 cm) length ginger
Green part of a leek or green onion
1 bay leaf
1 tablespoon sake
Chinese five-spice powder, cumin, sansho pepper or cilantro leaves, if desired

FOR THE CELERY CHUTNEY

1 tablespoon vegetable oil
1 stalk celery
½ garlic clove, minced
½ inch (1 cm) length ginger, minced
1 red chili pepper, stem and seeds removed
½ tablespoon doubanjiang spicy bean paste (available at Asian grocery stores)
½ tablespoon coarsely ground black pepper

SEASONING MIX

1 teaspoon salt
2 teaspoons sugar
½ tablespoon soy sauce

1 Cut the pork belly into ¾ inch (1.5 cm) cubes, and put into a pan with enough water to cover. Bring to a boil and drain off the water.

2 Rinse the pan and the pork quickly. Return the pork to the rinsed pan with the 4 cups (1 liter) water, the ginger and the leek, and set over high heat. When the pan comes to a boil, lower the heat and simmer gently until the meat is tender, about an hour to an hour and a half. Allow to cool, then refrigerate overnight. Remove the fat on the surface of the cooking liquid.

3 Measure the remaining cooking liquid. If it's more than 1½ cups (350 ml), cook it down; if it's less, add enough water to bring it up to that amount.

4 To make the celery chutney, heat the vegetable oil in a pan, add the rest of the chutney ingredients and stir-fry. When fragrant, add the Step 3 cooking liquid, the bay leaf, the cooked pork belly and the sake. When the mixture comes to a boil, add the seasoning mix. Leave as-is until cooled; heat up before serving for the best flavor. Sprinkle Chinese five-spice powder, cumin or sansho pepper to taste before serving. Alternatively, top with some roughly chopped cilantro.

Nihonshu-ya

Beautiful Small-Plate Dishes Made in Advance

Ever since it opened in 2009, this ambitious establishment has continually challenged preconceptions about Japanese sake. The small-plate dishes are exceptionally beautiful, adding visual appeal to their great taste.

With good seasoning, you don't need technique

In my restaurant we use wild-caught fish, and we buy our produce directly from farmers. Because the main ingredients have such a strong presence, they taste better without the addition of a lot of seasonings. It may be difficult to get such high-quality products to cook with at home, but you should at least try to obtain top-quality seasoning ingredients. For example, don't use "mirin seasoning," use real mirin. Don't use cooking sake containing additives—instead, use *junmai* pure rice sake or another drinking-quality sake. Did you know that, during the Edo period (1603–1868), mirin was considered to be a healthy drink? It's difficult to imagine making great-tasting food if you use a mirin that isn't good enough to drink on its own. Even if you spend a little extra money on your seasoning ingredients, they last a long time. Your cooking technique may be average, but just upgrading your seasonings will make your food taste amazing—that seems like a great trade-off. I believe this is a simple and effective way to make home cooking taste really good.

Keep an open, easygoing mindset

Because, as I mentioned above, my restaurant has the basic ingredients shipped to us directly from the producers, we never know what we're going to get. This means that the day's menu is decided based on what we have in front of us. If you think about it, regional cuisine is basically food that comes of figuring out what to make with ingredients that are abundant in any given location. Imagine that, in your region, a certain ingredient might not be available—so you would make it with a different one. That's how dishes unique to a region are devised. That's how cultures are created. In my restaurant, even if I think it would be nice to have a particular ingredient, I don't go out to buy it. Instead, I use what I have on hand—even if it's not perfectly suited to the dish. When you're

cooking at home, just because you don't have potatoes, pork and shirataki noodles on hand doesn't mean you can't make a version of *niku-jaga*, simmered meat and potatoes. You can use chicken instead of pork, and taro root instead of potatoes. Nikujaga itself may have originally been created because those happened to be the ingredients that were available. If you approach it this way, cooking is very freeing. You can just relax and enjoy it!

Recipes are like the sparks that make you want to eat a certain dish. It's okay if you don't follow them to the letter. If you look at cooking around the world, the way people do things is not that different: flavors are based on saltiness and sweetness combined with oil. So you can try using olive oil instead of sesa-me oil, or fish sauce instead of soy sauce. Just using a new seasoning in place of the one you usually use will result in an entirely new flavor. This is one way to make your homemade small plates more interesting.

Tips from Chef Takaya of Nihonshu-ya

1. Use seasoning ingredients that taste good on their own

The basic requirement for selecting your seasoning ingredi-ents is to choose products that taste good when you sip or taste them on their own. With soy sauce or salt, for exam-ple, when you put them on your tongue to compare them, you will discover some that aren't harsh, that have a well rounded flavor and a complexity to them.

2. You don't need to follow a recipe exactly

Recipes are not textbooks, so it's not wrong to depart from them somewhat. If you try out various things, even if they don't work, you might make new discoveries in the process. I think you should enjoy that journey.

3. Try switching up the ingredients or seasonings.

Don't be scared to substitute Japanese ingredients with ones that are easier for you to source. Try using fresh basil instead of green shiso, or lime instead of sudachi citrus. Use olive oil instead of sesame oil.

Umeboshi Plum with Enoki Mushrooms

This dish was designed to go well with Japanese sake. Since sake has a lot of umami and sweetness, it's a good companion for piquant foods like this. Leftovers will keep in the refrigerator for about 7 days.

Serves 4

7 oz (200 g) enoki mushrooms
1 umeboshi salt-pickled plum
4 tablespoons kombu dashi stock
2 tablespoons mirin
1 tablespoon vinegar
1 teaspoon light soy sauce
Large handful shredded bonito flakes
Shredded green shiso leaves, for garnish
Toasted sesame seeds, for garnish

1 Remove and discard the root ends from the enoki mushrooms and cut the mushrooms into 1 inch (2.5 cm) pieces. Remove and reserve the umeboshi pit; chop the pulp into a paste.
2 Combine the mushrooms, umeboshi pulp and reserved pit, kombu dashi, mirin, vinegar and soy sauce in a saucepan and bring to a simmer over medium heat. When the liquid has reduced and become somewhat thick, turn off the heat, remove the umeboshi pit, and add the bonito flakes.
3 Transfer to a serving bowl and top with the shiso and sesame seeds.

Chicken Wings with Spicy Miso Glaze

This is a chicken version of an Okinawan dish that coats simmered pork trotters with a spicy miso-vinegar sauce. Using chicken wings instead really brings out the delicious firm texture of the skin and meat. Leftovers will keep in the refrigerator for about 7 days. (When storing in the refrigerator, remove the bones and the wing tips first.)

Serves 4

8 chicken wing "flats" (middle parts) and tips
2¾ cups (650 ml) water, divided
2 teaspoons salt, divided
1 small Japanese or Asian cucumber

FOR THE MISO-VINEGAR SAUCE
2 tablespoons miso
1 tablespoons rice vinegar
Doubanjiang spicy bean paste, to taste
Garlic, to taste

1 Make an incision along the bone of the chicken wing and remove the bone from the meat (you can use scissors). If the wing tips are still attached, remove them as well. Reserve the bones and wing tips.
2 Put the chicken meat, bones and wing tips in a pan. Add 1¾ cups (400 ml) of the water and 1½ teaspoons of the salt. Bring to a boil, lower the heat and simmer slowly for about one and a half hours. Allow to cool in the cooking liquid.
3 Combine all the miso-vinegar sauce ingredients.
4 Slice the cucumber thinly, leaving every few slices attached. Mix the remaining 1 cup (250 ml) water and ½ teaspoon salt and soak the cucumber until wilted.
5 Arrange the chicken and cucumber on a serving plate and spoon the sauce over.

Avocado Marinated in Sake Lees

Miso and sake lees make a very versatile marinade paste that can be used for meat or fish, as well as for the avocado in this recipe. You can find sake lees at a Japanese or Asian grocery, or at a sake brewery, if you happen to live near one. For more information about sake lees, see page 39. The marinated avocado will keep in the refrigerator for about 3 days.

Serves 4

2½ tablespoons miso
2⅓ oz (70 g) sake lees (see note below)
½ firm avocado

1 Mix together the miso and sake lees to make a marinade paste.
2 Peel the avocado, halve it and remove the pit. Spread some of marinade paste on a piece of cling film with a rubber spatula, place the avocado halves on it and wrap it up. Marinate in the refrigerator overnight.
3 Wipe the marinade off the avocado and cut into pieces.

NOTE If you can, instead of the usual white sake lees, use brown sake lees that have been allowed to mature at room temperature. When they are aged in this way, sake lees become very fragrant and lose their alcoholic odor.

Chilled Tofu with Dashi Sauce

This is a variation on the chilled tofu seasoned with soy sauce that is a common bar snack in Japan. At first glance, this may appear to be an unseasoned block of tofu, but every bite of this deceptively simple dish is filled with savory umami.

Serves 4

1 block firm tofu, about 12 oz (350 g)
Thinly sliced myoga ginger and minced green onion, for garnish

FOR THE SAUCE
2 cups (500 ml) well-steeped dashi stock (see page 54)
1¾ teaspoons salt
6½ tablespoons mirin

1 Combine all the sauce ingredients in a pan and bring to a boil.
2 Lower the heat to medium and add the tofu. When the tofu is warmed through, turn off the heat. Allow to cool in the pan, then transfer to a storage container and refrigerate overnight.
3 Cut into pieces and serve topped with the myoga ginger and green onion. Pour some of the sauce onto the serving plate.

Simmered Sea Eel

The key to cooking sea eel (*anago* in Japanese) is to blanch and then rinse it to remove the surface sliminess completely. Here I have used palm-sized sea eels called *mesokko*. Other oily fish like small fresh mackerel or sardines may be used if sea eel is difficult to find.

Serves 4

4 to 5 small sea eels, about 10½ oz (300 g) total
Grated wasabi, for garnish

FOR THE SAUCE
1¼ cups (300 ml) water
6 tablespoons mirin
3 tablespoons sake
3 tablespoons soy sauce
1 tablespoon sugar (use beet sugar if possible)

1 Bring a pan of water to a boil. Add the eels and blanch for about a minute. Rinse under running water to remove the sliminess on the skin.
2 Combine all the sauce ingredients in a pan and bring to a boil. Add the blanched and rinsed eel, return to a boil and then turn the heat to low and simmer for about 20 minutes. Allow to cool in the sauce.
3 Cut into bite-sized pieces and top with a small mound of grated wasabi to serve.

Eggplant in Dashi Sauce

The key is to retain some firmness when deep-frying the eggplant—a bamboo skewer poked into it should encounter a little resistance, but the middle should not be hard or uncooked. Leftovers will keep in the refrigerator for 2 to 3 days.

Serves 4

3 to 5 small Asian or Japanese eggplants
Vegetable oil for deep-frying
Slivered myoga ginger buds or young ginger, for garnish

FOR THE DASHI SAUCE
2 cups (500 ml) dashi stock (see page 54), or niboshi dashi if possible
5½ tablespoons light soy sauce
5½ tablespoons mirin

1 Combine all the dashi sauce ingredients in a pan and bring to a boil. Remove from the heat and allow to cool.
2 If the eggplants are thick, make slits in the skin in a few places so that the heat penetrates easily. Pour 3 inches (7.5 cm) of the vegetable oil into a heavy pan or pot and heat to 360°F (180°C). Prepare a bowl of ice water. Deep-fry the eggplant. When a skewer passes through one with just a little resistance, remove the eggplant from the oil and dunk it immediately in the ice water. This fixes the bright purple color.
3 Drain the eggplant very well and transfer to a storage container. Pour the sauce over and marinate in the refrigerator for several hours.
4 Cut the eggplant into bite-sized pieces. Serve topped with the slivered myoga ginger or young ginger.

Miso-Marinated Sweet Onion

The dill, mint, and white wine in this simple dish add a European touch. If you want the chopped herbs to keep their color, you can add them just before serving instead of mixing them with the marinade.

Serves 4

1 sprig fresh dill
A few mint leaves
1 sweet onion
Salt, for sprinkling

FOR THE MISO MARINADE
6 tablespoons miso
1 tablespoon + 2 teaspoons mirin
1 tablespoon + 2 teaspoons white wine

1 Remove the tough stem from the dill and chop the dill leaves roughly with the mint leaves. Mix all the miso marinade ingredients together. Add the dill and mint.
2 Cut the onion into ½ inch (1 cm) wedges. Sprinkle with a little salt and allow to sweat for a while.
3 Pat the excess moisture off the onions. Mix to coat with the miso marinade and refrigerate overnight. Serve as-is.

Soybean Hummus

Instead of the usual chickpeas, I have used soybeans here, which impart a subtle Japanese flavor to this hummus. It's delicious served alongside meat or fish or as a small-plate dish with bread. This easy-to-make amount will keep in the refrigerator for about 7 days.

Serves 4

3½ oz (100 g) dried soybeans
½ garlic clove, grated
2 teaspoons tahini
2 tablespoons + 1 teaspoon heavy cream
Salt, to taste
Olive oil, to taste
Ground paprika, for garnish, optional

1 Put the dry soybeans in a pan with plenty of water. Do not soak; bring directly to a boil and then simmer for about an hour until they are cooked but still quite firm.
2 Drain the beans, reserving the cooking liquid. Put the beans in a food processor and add the garlic, tahini and cream. Process, adding the reserved cooking liquid a little at a time until the hummus reaches your preferred consistency. Season with salt to taste.
3 Transfer to a serving plate and pour olive oil over. Sprinkle with paprika if desired.

Mini Chicken Hot Pot

It's important to use bone-in chicken for this, and to simmer it for a long time until the broth turns white. Use vegetables of your choice—for the dish in the photo, I used blanched bok choy and steamed, peeled eggplant. It's also delicious with some Thai fish sauce sprinkled on top. Leftovers will keep in the refrigerator for about 2 days.

Serves 4

4 bone-in chicken thighs, about 1 lb 2 oz (500 g) total, cut into pieces
Cooked vegetables of your choice
Salt, to taste
Ponzu soy sauce (see page 16), to taste
Yuzu kosho paste, to taste

1 Put about 3 quarts (3 liters) of water in a large pan with the chicken over medium-high heat. Simmer for about 3 hours until the liquid is white and cloudy. If the water boils down too much while it's cooking, add some more.
2 Cut the vegetables into bite-sized pieces. Add them to the pan and cook until heated through. Add salt to taste.
3 Serve with ponzu soy sauce and yuzu kosho paste.

Brandade

This simple dish combining white fish with potatoes really allows you to taste each ingredient. My recipe uses fresh fish instead of the traditional salt cod. For a richer flavor, use cream and butter instead of milk and olive oil. Leftovers will keep in the refrigerator for 4 to 5 days.

Serves 4

14 oz (400 g) potatoes
7 oz (200 g) cod or other fresh white fish
1 clove garlic, peeled
Milk, for simmering fish
Salt, to taste
Pink peppercorns, optional
4 slices good bread
Olive oil, for drizzling

1 Put the potatoes in a pan and add enough water to cover. Boil until a skewer goes through one easily. Drain and peel.
2 Put the fish and garlic in a separate pan and add enough milk to cover. Simmer until the garlic is soft. Take the fish and garlic out of the pan, reserving the simmering liquid. Remove the bones and skin from the fish.
3 Put the potatoes, fish and garlic in a food processor. Add the reserved simmering liquid a little at a time and process to your preferred consistency. The puree should not be too loose. Season to taste with salt.
4 Arrange on a plate and top with pink peppercorns if desired. To eat, spread on the bread and drizzle with olive oil.

Ratatouille with Poached Egg

This classic dish is easy to make and allows you to use up a lot of vegetables in the summer. Eat it topped with a poached egg and grated Parmesan for extra flavor. The ratatouille will keep in the refrigerator for about 3 days.

Serves 4

14 oz (400 g) summer vegetables such as eggplant, peppers, and zucchini, in any combination
½ onion (about 3½ oz / 100 g total)
2 sticks celery
1 clove garlic
2 tablespoons olive oil
14 oz (400 g) canned whole tomatoes
1⅔ cups (400 ml) water
Salt, to taste
4 eggs
1 tablespoon vinegar
Parmesan cheese
Coarsely ground black pepper

1 Cut the summer vegetables into bite-sized pieces. Mince the onion, celery and garlic.

2 Heat the olive oil in a pan and sauté the garlic over medium heat until fragrant. Add the onion and celery and continue sautéing. When the onion is translucent, add the canned tomatoes and the water and simmer, uncovered, over medium heat. When there is just a little liquid left in the pan, add the summer vegetables and continue simmering until everything is soft. Add salt to taste.

3 To poach the eggs, bring a pan of water to a boil and add the vinegar to the water. Crack one egg into a small bowl. Lower the heat and gently ease the egg into the simmering water. Swirl the water around the edge of the pan to keep the white around the yolk. When the white has firmed up, remove with a slotted spoon and place on a wadded-up paper towel to drain. Repeat with remaining eggs.

4 Arrange the ratatouille on plates and top each plate with a poached egg. Grate some Parmesan over and sprinkle with black pepper.

Japanese-Style Roast Beef

This dish takes its inspiration from the salty-sweet duck that's served at soba restaurants. If you sear and seal the surface of the beef, all you need to do is to submerge it in the hot marinade to finish. The seared beef in the marinade will keep for 4 to 5 days if refrigerated.

Serves 4

14 oz (400 g) beef rump or round
1 teaspoon vegetable oil
5–6 salt-pickled green peppercorns, optional

FOR THE MARINADE
⅞ cup (200 ml) mirin
⅞ cup (200 ml) sake
⅔ cup (150 ml) soy sauce
A few brown cardamom pods, or star anise, whole cloves or black cardamom

1 Cut the beef into 4 pieces of approximately equal weight. Let stand at room temperature until the meat is no longer cold.
2 Heat the vegetable oil in a skillet over medium heat. Sear the beef on all sides until it changes color.
3 Combine all the marinade ingredients in a saucepan and bring to a boil. Add the beef and cover the pan with a lid. Remove the pan from the heat and leave the beef for about an hour so that it continues to cook in the residual heat and absorbs the flavors of the marinade.
4 Slice the beef thinly and arrange on a serving dish with a little marinade. Sprinkle with pickled green peppercorns, if desired.

About the Izakayas

Here are the details for the six izakayas whose recipes are featured in this book.
All are small jewels where you can enjoy talking to the owner-chef across the counter.
Please enjoy the care and pride each chef takes in their drinks and their food.

Kotaro

From delicate small vegetable dishes to hearty deep-fried meatballs, a wide variety of Japanese-style small plates are served. Since there's no partition between the counter and the kitchen, it's fun to communicate freely with friendly Chef Hayashi and his staff.

28-2 Sakuraoka-cho
Mikasa Bldg, 1st Floor
Shibuya, Tokyo
Tel: 03-5438-5705
Hours: 18:00 - 24:00 (last order: 23:00)
Closed on Sundays and the first Monday of the month

Ametsuchi

A variety of dishes bring out the lively flavors of seasonal vegetables are served here. The comforting food and relaxed environment truly reflects the personality of the owner, Chef Tsuchii.

1-35-7 Naka-cho
Meguro, Tokyo
Tel: 03-3712-1806
Hours: 18:00 - 23:00 Tue-Fri (last order: 22:00); 17:00 - 22:00 Sat-Sun (last order: 21:00)
Closed Mondays, the second and fourth Tuesday of the month, and some national holidays

Shuko Takigiya

When you make your way through the noren curtains at the entrance, get ready to enjoy the homemade dried fish and simmered seasonal vegetables that are this restaurant's specialty. Enjoy the carefully selected choice of premium sakes that pair so well with the dishes served here.

7 Araki-cho
Ando Bldg, 1st floor
Shinjuku, Tokyo
Tel: 03-3351-1776
Hours: 17:00 - 23:30 (last order); Sat. 17:00 - 22:30 (last order)
Closed Sundays, national holidays

Shutei Zorome

"A merging of old and new" is the theme here, where seasonality and the inspiration that comes from the owner's travels are incorporated into the cooking. There are more than 60 items served every day, ranging from fresh seafood to gyoza dumplings.

1-12-6 Tomioka
Akutsu Bldg. 1st floor
Koto, Tokyo
Tel: 03-5675-8382
Hours: 17:00 - 1:00
Closed Sundays

Sakebozu

This establishment has such an exotic atmosphere it's hard to believe that it's a Japanese izakaya. As befits the setting, you can enjoy sake and food combinations that exceed your imagination. The subtle use of spices is really nice.

1-37-1 Tomigaya
Rona-YS Bldg. 201
Shibuya, Tokyo
Tel: 03-3466-1311
Hours: 16:00 - 23:00; Sun and national holidays 14:00 - 21:00
Closed occasionally

Nihonshu-ya

"The sake is the base point, and the cooking revolves around it" is the philosophy of Chef Takaya, and this thinking permeates everything he does. You can enjoy dishes that aren't constrained by Japanese tradition here, as well as great sake pairings.

2-7-13 Kichijoji Honcho
Ladybird Bldg. 101
Musashino, Tokyo
Tel: 0422-20-1722
Hours: 17:00 - 24:00
Sat., Sun and national holidays 13:00 - 24:00
Closed Thursdays

Index of Recipes by Main Ingredient

"Books to Span the East and West"

Tuttle Publishing was founded in 1832 in the small New England town of Rutland, Vermont [USA]. Our core values remain as strong today as they were then—to publish best-in-class books which bring people together one page at a time. In 1948, we established a publishing office in Japan—and Tuttle is now a leader in publishing English-language books about the arts, languages and cultures of Asia. The world has become a much smaller place today and Asia's economic and cultural influence has grown. Yet the need for meaningful dialogue and information about this diverse region has never been greater. Over the past seven decades, Tuttle has published thousands of books on subjects ranging from martial arts and paper crafts to language learning and literature—and our talented authors, illustrators, designers and photographers have won many prestigious awards. We welcome you to explore the wealth of information available on Asia at **www.tuttlepublishing.com**.

Published by Tuttle Publishing, an imprint of
Periplus Editions (HK) Ltd.

www.tuttlepublishing.com

CHIISANA MEITEN NO KANBAN TSUMAMI

ISBN: 978-4-8053-1700-6

25 24 23 22

10 9 8 7 6 5 4 3 2 1

Printed in China 2204EP

Distributed by
North America, Latin America & Europe
Tuttle Publishing
364 Innovation Drive
North Clarendon, VT 05759-9436 U.S.A.
Tel: 1 (802) 773-8930
Fax: 1 (802) 773-6993
info@tuttlepublishing.com
www.tuttlepublishing.com

Japan
Tuttle Publishing
Yaekari Building 3rd Floor
5-4-12 Osaki
Shinagawa-ku
Tokyo 141-0032
Tel: (81) 3 5437-0171
Fax: (81) 3 5437-0755
sales@tuttle.co.jp
www.tuttle.co.jp

Asia Pacific
Berkeley Books Pte. Ltd.
3 Kallang Sector #04-01
Singapore 349278
Tel: (65) 6741 2178
Fax: (65) 6741 2179
inquiries@periplus.com.sg
www.tuttlepublishing.com